D1206091

*The Wheel of Servitude*

# The Wheel of Servitude

## Black Forced Labor after Slavery

Daniel A. Novak

*The University Press of Kentucky*

ISBN: 0-8131-1371-7

Library of Congress Catalog Card Number: 77-76334

Copyright © 1978 by The University Press of Kentucky

A statewide cooperative scholarly publishing agency
serving Berea College, Centre College of Kentucky,
Eastern Kentucky University, The Filson Club,
Georgetown College, Kentucky Historical Society,
Kentucky State University, Morehead State University,
Murray State University, Northern Kentucky University,
Transylvania University, University of Kentucky,
University of Louisville, and Western Kentucky University.

*Editorial and Sales Offices*: Lexington, Kentucky 40506

To John P. Roche

# Contents

# Foreword

The history of American blacks between the end of slavery and the beginning of the modern civil rights movement has been sadly neglected. In contrast, the publication of Kenneth Stampp's *The Peculiar Institution* in 1956 sparked a renaissance of scholarship in the sociology, psychology, history, and economics of slavery. The new research, challenging insights, and novel theories of Stanley Elkins, Herbert Gutman, Eugene Genovese, Robert Fogel, Stanley Engerman, and others has ignited scholarly and popular controversy. But if one result of the renewed interest in slavery has been an enriched understanding of an extraordinarily important period in the evolution of American race relations, considerable confusion is a by-product. The problem is not that the theories of this or that scholar have a pernicious effect on public attitudes or policy. Rather it is that this renewed interest reinforces the tendency to reduce the history of American blacks to the history of slavery. It is widely assumed, perhaps unconsciously, that the proper understanding of slavery holds the key to the recovery of our cities, to the solution of the welfare crisis, and even to the ending of racial discrimination and inequality. Although slavery is clearly the basis for all future developments of relations between the races, it does not and cannot explain everything. A fuller and more accurate history of slavery is essential, but our understanding will be restricted and incomplete until and unless we have an equal grasp of the history of the American black following emancipation.

Daniel Novak's *The Wheel of Servitude: Black Forced Labor after Slavery* is, thus, of more than intrinsic importance and interest. It is an indication that a new generation of scholars may be beginning to recognize the importance of this neglected period in American history. Although Novak's work is primarily a legal study, it is filled with important insights into the new economic and social system that replaced slavery. It provides much-needed perspectives on the postslavery South that will be of interest not only to professional historians, but also to everyone who is concerned with understanding the historical and social development of racism and race relations in the United States.

While the failure of Reconstruction, radical or otherwise, to establish a strong and secure basis for black freedom and equality by economically transforming southern society is well known, much less attention has been given to trying to understand what replaced slavery. The usual concentration upon the politics of the Radical legislatures has, if anything, directed attention away from the more critical questions of economic relationships that replaced slavery. Daniel Novak builds a convincing case that the new system had much in common with slavery: the old fugitive slave laws were reborn, and the convict-labor system quoted prices for classes of prisoners which were taken directly from the terminology of slavery. His detailed examination of the laws governing labor relations in the postwar South yields a stark and depressing picture of a new social and economic system that continued the oppression and degradation of black workers. As legally defined, the new system closely paralleled serfdom. In fact, Novak observes, compared to the medieval serf the freed Negro had considerably less legal protection, while the control of his movements was at least as great.

The accepted wisdom that the entrenchment of Jim Crow was primarily the result of the withdrawal of federal troops from the South following the compromise of 1877 is persuasively challenged by Novak. He points out that not only did the federal government fail to reconstruct the South, but that it can accurately be described as a partner in the creation of the new system. It was the Freedmen's Bureau, not southern bourbons or the Ku Klux Klan, which initiated and enforced the regulations that became models for the Black Codes, the legal foundation and reflection of the new system of forced labor. Although the bureau and the army did try, within limits, to protect the rights of the freedman, they basically supported the emerging system of control.

Even more surprisingly, not a single radical southern legislature became involved in the labor field in a way that might have, however briefly, destroyed the peonage system set up by the Black Codes and the Freedmen's Bureau. Radicalism was restricted to issues like suffrage, segregation, and education, while legislation on labor remained essentially conservative. Thus, during the period when radicalism supposedly ran rampant over the defeated South, something far different was happening. As Novak writes, "the newly freed agricultural worker was, by *consensus*, placed in a position of peonage."

*The Wheel of Servitude* suggests that economics, especially the forced labor system, must be placed at the center of the historian's vision if we are to understand southern history. In Novak's hands this approach yields valuable insights into the nature of the Populist movement and the reasons for its failure. The Populist movement virtually ignored the needs of agrarians caught in the trap of sharecropping and wage labor, the positions occupied by the overwhelming majority of Negro farmers. This was not accidental, according to Novak, for the Populist movement was based upon property-owning farmers. Thus, it is not surprising that Populism did not fundamentally challenge the southern system.

The great value of Daniel Novak's *The Wheel of Servitude* is, however, the clarity he brings to explaining the legal mechanisms that reenslaved the newly freed blacks and to discussing how the laws reflected the dependence of the southern economy upon a system of forced labor. Changes in the lien laws, for instance, are convincingly explained here as a response to the growth of sharecropping and tenantry as alternatives to wage labor.

*The Wheel of Servitude* is of more than historical interest. In one sense, it is a case study of the centrality of economics to the progress of social justice. More important, as Novak reminds us, peonage is a current issue. Cases of peonage have been reported in North Carolina and Florida during the summer of 1977 and there is no doubt that even today this form of near slavery is a great deal more extensive than most Americans would like to believe.

Both scholars and social activists will be richly rewarded by reading this illuminating study of a critical and little-understood period in American history, a study that traces the connections between the southern legal structures and the new system of labor control that emerged in the aftermath of the Civil War.

BAYARD RUSTIN

# Acknowledgments

The idea of examining black contract labor laws was first put into my head by my friend and mentor John P. Roche. Professor Roche offered me encouragement, advice, and, most important, his exceptional capacity for cutting through to the heart of any problem. He has been the Virgil of my infernal graduate travels into the purgatory of junior academe. John T. Eliff assisted me in the later stages of preparation, making available relevant materials in his possession and some sound practical advice. My colleague, Professor Richard Ellis, criticized the manuscript with care and good sense and has earned my gratitude and affection. His kaffeeklatsch analyses remain a bright spot in my day. I should also like to thank James Eaglin for his help in the preparation of this study.

The James Gordon Foundation of Brandeis University, through its financial support, gave me the time fully to devote myself to this research. The A. Philip Randolph Foundation, the David Dubinsky Foundation, and the Faculty of Social Sciences and Administration of the State University of New York at Buffalo have been kind enough to support the publication of this manuscript. Brandeis University, where I completed my graduate studies, holds a special place in my affections; the generous support provided by the Chancellor's Fund can only serve to confirm and enlarge this feeling.

Professor Stanley Feingold of the City College of New York first introduced me to the twin fascinations of law and politics. Our subsequent friendship, and the strength of affection between our families (with the inexplicable exception of my dog), is a constant pleasure. As in all things, my wife, Josephine, was my mainstay and support in the preparation of this study. A tough critic and stalwart grammarian, she is responsible for those sections of the manuscript which meet the standards of English usage. None of this would have been possible without her. My two sons, David and Jeremy, have, through the simple expedient of growing older, with a commensurate increase in appetite, made the completion of this work necessary.

# Introduction

*. . . labor contracts between the freedman and the landlords [were] a revolutionary reform more important in the actual life of the freedman than the sensational but largely unsuccessful political changes attempted at the time.*

*Francis B. Simkins*

Perhaps the most striking aspects of the study of peonage in the South are the dearth of widespread interest in the subject and the dogged resilience of the institution. The general indifference to the subject is all the more remarkable in light of the basic nature of the practice. It was a simple and effective substitute for the previous system of labor control—slavery. Brutal as it was, peonage was, concededly, no match for its predecessor; but the elements of violence present, combined with the rigorous control of its victims, should have been prime sources of study. Without fanfare the freed slave was plunged into a new labor system that degraded his value as a worker and made his new freedom a mockery, in economic terms at least. Yet this new system replaced the old, not only without significant outcry, but with the assistance or acceptance of those forces one would have expected to be in the forefront of the opposition: the federal government and the "radical" Reconstruction legislatures.

Even in later years, when the "Negro revolution" was in full swing, peonage took a back seat. The emphasis of this revolution has been on the reacquisition of the rights originally present after emancipation. Suffrage; desegregation of schools, transport, and public accommodations; the right to jury service—in short, those elements that we have come to call civil rights—are at the center of the action. It is not unreasonable to expect that civil rights leaders and historians would concentrate on these rights and how they were suppressed over the years. The highly symbolic nature of these rights in a democracy makes for added

interest. Further, the story is filled with the romance and revulsion of the white-sheeted Klan and the duplicity of northern
politicians. The fact that these rights had been acquired by law
and were removed by terror infuses this history with an aura of
drama. Clearly, the story of the agricultural contract laborers,
whose rights were severely circumscribed even at the height of
Reconstruction, presents a far less juicy area of attack. Rights
that have never been given, laws and customs that have remained relatively consistent throughout postbellum southern
history, seem to suggest a sort of consensus that the situation is
somehow justified and reasonable.

This very continuity of law and practice, on the other hand,
itself poses an intriguing question. How has this practice re-
tained its viability over the years? Here other factors come into
play—for example, the difficulty of affecting ingrained social
practices through law, and the presence of economic pressures
as a spur to opponents of reform and as a bar to effective
enforcement.

Before one can discuss these questions, however, it is necessary to recount the history of peonage. In view of the lack of any
definitive studies of the subject, a survey of that history, from the
end of the Civil War to the present, is presented here. There is
one major study of southern peonage: Pete Daniel, *Shadow of
Slavery: Peonage in the South, 1901–1969* (Urbana: University of
Illinois Press, 1972). But Daniel deals only with the period after
1900, ignoring the critical beginnings of the practice. In addition, he is writing a social rather than a legal study of peonage,
and he concentrates his efforts on telling the full stories of a few
significant incidents of the practice in that period. A realistic picture could not be drawn through an intensive study of the practice in any one southern state; although it is true that, generally,
practices varied only cosmetically, in the absence of supportive
secondary sources it has been necessary to demonstrate that fact.
Further, the questions raised require the researcher to trace the
patterns of peonage through the years, as practices and legal
issues change. Although the survey cannot be comprehensive, it
does touch all those areas which seemed relevant.

In essence, this is a legal study. Rather than concentrate on the
anecdotal material on peonage—that is, the brutal and often

sensational stories of its victims—the writer has chosen to treat the topic as a legal issue. Thus, the major emphasis will be on the development and implementation of the laws which have supported (and those which theoretically should have destroyed) this obnoxious spawn of slavery.

The subject is dealt with chronologically; each chapter, with the exception of the conclusion, deals with a defined historical period. In the conclusion the questions raised here are dealt with in some greater detail. Finally, a brief bibliography discusses the historiography of Reconstruction and of peonage.

The reader should be warned that, although peonage has a distinct legal meaning (i.e., debt-slavery), it will generally be used here to describe any system of forced labor not under penal supervision. The legal definition is, in the writer's opinion, a misreading of an old statute. The legally precise meaning will, of course, be used when appropriate, as, for example, when discussing the limits of the Anti-Peonage Act vis-à-vis an Anti-Slavery Act.

# 1
# The Black Codes

*The nigger is going to be made a serf.*
*—Conversation of Alabama planters, 1865*

The Civil War marked the end of the great debate on slavery in practical political terms. The abolitionist position had been victorious, not through persuasion, but by force of arms. The slave economy of the Confederacy was destroyed and a new method of dealing with a vast work force had to be devised. Since the rationale behind the old system remained intact in the minds of the now dispossessed slave owners, it is not at all surprising that the initial response to this new situation was an attempt to retain as much of slavery as possible. This tendency is made clear by the creation of the "Black Codes," which seem intended to reproduce, within the new limits, a close approximation of the now forbidden master-slave relationship.

The first stage of the political reconstruction of the South took place under the supervision of Presidents Lincoln and Johnson. From 1864 until 1867, when Congress took over the job, presidential Reconstruction left the South relatively free from interference from the federal government, save for the requirement that emancipation take place. Under Lincoln's plan, when 10 percent of the prewar voting population of a state had taken an oath of allegiance to the Union, they might proceed to form a new government. This was changed by Johnson (who excluded some of the wealthier old landowning classes from participation), but in this area his general thrust was the same. Therefore, shortly after the end of the war, the Confederacy had "reconstructed" itself with new state legislatures and administrations. It should be made clear, however, that the new legislators were, by and large, the same men who had run the Old South, or at least they reflected its values. This orientation was made evident by the Black Codes they quickly enacted.

Mississippi, in the first of the postwar constitutional conventions, immediately got down to the problem that was uppermost in the minds of white southerners: "The institution of slavery having been destroyed . . . the legislature at its next session . . . shall provide by law for the protection and security of the person and property of the freedmen of the state, and guard them and the State against any evil that may arise from their sudden emancipation."[1]

Since this phrase was copied, in some cases verbatim, by the other states, it is clear that the significance of the language was not lost on the Radicals in and out of Congress. Even some modern southern historians claim that the North, and especially the northern press, overreacted to these phrases, but in view of the legislation that followed, it is difficult to sustain this position.

The "legislation concerning the freed negro" which emerged from the "reconstructed" states of the Confederacy in 1865 and 1866 made it clear that the white South had no intention of dealing with a truly free black labor force. With formal slavery barred, a complex of laws setting up a system of peonage or debt slavery was formulated to fill the gap.

Short-lived though they were, at least with regard to their specifically discriminatory wording, the codes presaged the system under which the black agricultural laborer was to be bound in later years. For the purposes of this study, only those provisions relating to the imposition of forced labor will be examined, although the remaining sections of the codes make fascinating reading by themselves.

Mississippi's opening effort, ironically titled "An Act to confer Civil Rights on Freedmen," barred the freedman from renting land outside city limits, thus ensuring that blacks could not begin farming on their own. Further, by the following January, and annually thereafter, each freedman had to hold written proof of lawful employment (i.e., a labor contract). The absence of such evidence was prima facie proof of vagrancy. Should a freedman breach his contract "without good cause," he was subject to arrest by the police or other civil officer. The arresting officer was entitled to a reward of five dollars (plus ten cents per mile traveled), to be paid out of the laborer's wages. As a further insurance against flight, the old Fugitive Slave Laws were reborn: any person attempting to "entice" a laborer from his master, employ him, or otherwise aid or harbor him was subject to criminal as well as civil penalties.[2]

It should be noted here that this last provision represented an innovation in American law. Although simple breach of contract by free labor was traditionally subject to civil action only (except when sailors jumped ship), there was some precedent for the imposition of criminal penalties in Anglo-American law; indeed, such penalties could be imposed in England until the passage of the 1875 Employers and Workman's Act.[3] Enticement of a servant, however, has never been a criminal offense at common law.[4]

The next act passed by the legislature dealt with "Master and Apprentice" relationships "as relates to Freedmen, Free Negroes and Mulattoes." It allowed the probate courts to apprentice any black child whose parents could not or would not support him. First preference in the assignment of masters should go to "the former owner of said minors."[5]

In its new vagrancy law, Mississippi broadened the previous definitions to include runaways, persons lewd in speech or behavior, those who misspend their earnings or neglect their work, and all other idle or disorderly persons. Further, idle blacks, and whites who "associated with them on terms of equality" or had sexual relations with them, were similarly classified as vagrants. A white person could evade the fine by taking a pauper's oath, but a black could be hired out at auction in order to pay his fine and costs. To ensure adequate enforcement, justices of the peace, mayors, and aldermen were given jurisdiction to try such crimes.[6]

This act also authorized a "head" tax on all Negroes between the ages of eighteen and sixty, and failure to pay was prima facie evidence of vagrancy. Finally, an act which established new county courts provided that only blacks could be hired out to provide payment for their fines.[7]

The legislature enacted a number of other discriminatory bills not germane to this study, and finally, with a superb sense of propriety, finished its job by voting not to ratify the Thirteenth Amendment, which, after all, barred involuntary servitude.[8]

Thus came into law the first of the Black Codes. The reaction of the northern press and the federal officials in the state to this legislative package caused some bewilderment.[9] When General O. O. Howard, head of the Freedmen's Bureau, ordered the bureau's officers to disregard the codes, and General Thomas Wood issued an order forbidding prosecution of blacks under its provisions, the state was truly shocked.[10] There was, perhaps, some justice in this feeling, for both the Freedman's Bureau and the army had been enforcing similar restrictions on their own accounts.

South Carolina was by this time in the process of producing her own version of the Black Codes. Governor Orr, a newly elected and "presidentially reconstructed" official, urged the passage of the code, arguing that, while the freedmen must be protected in their rights and property (and from "the fraud . . . of the artful"), they must also be "restrained from theft, idleness, vagrancy and crime, and taught the *absolute necessity* of strictly complying with their contracts for labor."[11]

The basic elements of this latter "necessity" were contained in an act purporting to regulate "the Domestic Relations of Persons of Color." Once again, contracts were enforced by criminal sanctions, and laborers were required to get the master's written permission to leave the plantation or to have visitors. To ensure that the freedman was restricted to the plantation, no black man could operate a store or work as a craftsman without the approval of a district judge (essentially a justice of the peace), attesting to his fitness and moral character—and the payment of a "freedman's license" fee of up to one hundred dollars. A poll tax on all black males and unmarried black females was authorized, and failure to pay was evidence of vagrancy. Vagrancy itself was given the broadest possible definition, as in Mississippi, and the convicted vagrant could be hired out for the extent of the sentence. The apprenticeship sections gave the district courts the right to bind out the children of blacks who were idle or paupers, or who failed to teach their children "habits of industry and honesty."[12] Notably, the use of criminal penalties to prevent the enticement of a servant or his harboring was not included in the South Carolina codes at this time.

The military commander of the district, General David Sickles, declared the codes to be without force virtually upon their passage. Thus, the first two Black Codes, passed almost simultaneously, were wiped out with equivalent speed.[13]

Louisiana and Alabama were the next states to act. Louisiana produced legislation to make the labor of freedmen "available to the agricultural interests of the State."[14] Thus blacks had to contract for the year by the first of January, and breach of contract resulted in criminal penalties. Failure to have proof of contract was evidence of vagrancy.[15] The vagrancy law, which made no racial distinctions, was broadened in its compass, and provision was made for the hiring out of convicted vagrants (here an out was given to those who could convince a judge of their good behavior and future industry, obviously to provide a safety valve for convicted whites) and the penalty was raised from six months to a year. Enticement, harboring, or employing "runaway servants" was made a penal offense, and the legislature added a new twist, demanding that all employers be shown a written discharge from the laborer's former master.[16]

The local parishes and towns went further: in Bossier Parish, Saint Landry Parish and in the towns of Franklin and Opelousas, stringent regulations were passed. These required the freedman to have a permit to travel and barred him from renting or buying property and from entering town limits without the permission of his employer. In Franklin, passes from the "police jury" were required for practically every activity known to man, and in Bossier Parish a similar situation prevailed. These local provisions were nullified by the bureau and the military, but the state codes were allowed to stand.[17]

Alabama took moderate action compared to her sister states. An act defining a vagrant as any laborer who failed to "comply with any contract for a term of service without just cause" or any "runaway or stubborn servant" was atypical in that no reference was made to race. The enticement law followed the same pattern. However, the apprenticeship law did give preference to former owners in the binding out of the children of freedmen, whilst applying to children of any race.[18] An act to regulate and enforce labor contracts, passed by the legislature, was vetoed by the governor, apparently at the urging of General Swayne, the military commander of the district.[19]

All of the codes cited above were passed in 1865, and their adverse reception by the northern press, federal officials, and the like might have been taken as a warning by those states which had not yet acted. If Florida is any example, however, there was little impact. The legislative committee report on "legislation concerning the freedman" was quite spectacular. It proceeded from the premise that slavery was a "benign" institution "constituting the happiest and best provided-for laboring population in the world" and that "the only inherent evil of the institution of slavery, as it existed in the Southern States, was the inadequately regulated sex life of the negroes."[20] With this set of premises, it is easy to anticipate the committee's recommendations.

The Florida contract law punished breach by declaring the guilty laborer a prima facie vagrant. This same definition applied to any laborer convicted of "willful disobedience of orders . . . impudence . . . disrespect to his employer . . . [or] idleness." Of course, a convicted vagrant could be hired out for up to a year, if not imprisoned or whipped. In fact, any person not able to pay a fine, regardless of offense, *should* be hired out at public auction to cover the fine and costs.[21] None of these laws applied specifically to blacks, but their intended application was clear to all concerned. The contract law, for example, was made applicable only to agriculture and lumbering.

Georgia was somewhat less defiant and operated within the same context (i.e., her laws made no specific reference to race). The vagrancy law broadened the definition of the term, provided for the binding out of those convicted (without necessary reference to fines), and gave the usual escape clause for whites of posting a bond if the judge was convinced of the criminal's potential "good behavior and industry." An enticement law providing criminal sanctions was passed in the absence of a labor contract provision, which died in committee.[22]

Perhaps the most fascinating ploy used by the Georgia legislators was the reduction of a variety of crimes from felonies to misdemeanors, to some observers at least, a clear manifestation of southern beneficence. Its practical effect, however, was to permit the substitution of whipping for imprisonment and to expand the field of potential candidates for "hiring out."[23]

North Carolina and Virginia did not enact much significant legislation in this area; both passed vagrancy laws of the (by now) standard stripe, broadening the definition and providing for the hiring out of those convicted.[24] Apparently encouraged by the bureau, they stopped there.

Texas was the last state to enact a significant body of laws that fall under the heading of Black Codes. Acting cautiously, in the new pattern, no mention of race was made. The labor contract law provided no criminal penalties for breach, although it forbade visitors, made contracts cover the entire family of the worker, and instituted a fascinating system of fines; the fines, imposed by the employer at his discretion, were clearly capable of making the wage system a joke. The mildness of this law was countered by the vehemence of the enticement statute, which matched the best of the earlier codes in the stringency of its penalties and the inclusion of the "written proof of discharge" idea first introduced by the Louisiana code. The vagrancy act was relatively mild, for the felon could be put to work only by the town or county, and while police courts could hire out those convicted of misdemeanors, the term of service was restricted to the length of the sentence. Apprenticeship laws were stringent, but without reference to race or former masters.[25]

Tennessee took no action of significance, and Arkansas did not even bother to repeal its old slave laws until 1867.[26]

The laws cited in the preceding pages reflect, of course, only a few of the many aspects of the Black Codes. Those laws unrelated to the subject under study have been ignored, as have those totally on all fours with previously enacted legislation. In the end, the totality of the codes caused a major uproar in the North, with the newspapers screaming that they represented an open return to slavery. It seems difficult to argue with this view, but many historians have made the effort, denouncing the "agitators" of the northern press, who did not look at the problems of the South and failed to see the protections for freedmen inherent in the codes.

As the arguments in the legislatures make clear, however, the legislators themselves had no illusions on this point. Neither, needless to say, did the plantation owners. One planter put in a standing order with the local courts, announcing that he would take their entire output of criminals, and complaining about the sparse yield of his convenient employment agency.[27]

This interlaced construct of laws was the South's answer to the Thirteenth Amendment. It went straight to the heart of the matter, and it seems evident that the Alabama planters quoted at the beginning of this chapter knew what they were talking about. In fact, the control of the movements and labor of the freedman under the Black Codes was at least as great as that which governed the medieval serf.

# 2

# The Freedmen's Bureau
# and the Army

*. . . wholesome compulsion eventuated in larger independence.*
*General O. O. Howard*

In March 1864, President Lincoln signed a bill creating in the War Department a Bureau of Refugees, Freedmen and Abandoned Lands. It was to last for one year after the end of the war, and it was to supervise, manage, and control "all subjects relating to refugees and freedmen."[1] Basically, the bureau was to be the means of easing the passage of the black from slavery to freedom. In most Reconstruction histories, however, the bureau is depicted as the principal tool in the Radicals' conspiracy to subjugate the South. It is shown riding roughshod over civil justice, economic rights, and the basic rules of social decency.

In view of the historical record of its actions, the awesome reputation of the bureau surely represents an equally awesome historical misrepresentation. With regard to economics, in any case, "General O. O. Howard and the Misrepresented Bureau" enforced and supported the system of labor contracts which led to the establishment of black peonage.[2] In fact, even a rough scan of the records of the Freedmen's Bureau and the army makes clear that the Black Codes regulating labor were little more than local validations of the regulations initiated and enforced by the federal authorities.[3]

It must be conceded that the bureau and the army faced an unenviable task, providing a semblance of order amidst the ruins of a defeated culture. The army, first to face the problem, arrived at a "solution" without prompting. In a variety of locales, a variety of officers came to similar conclusions—namely, that their first job was to keep the freedman on the plantation and to keep him working. The freedman should stay on the farm of his former owner, gather the crops, and refrain from vagrancy, idleness, and wandering. Those who did not obey were to be arrested and forced to work in penal servitude. In fact, the first convict lease systems were initiated by military commanders in Georgia, Mississippi, and Louisiana.[4]

General Howard, head of the bureau, also felt the need to keep the former slave at work "down on the farm." However, to ensure that slavery was not reinstituted, he decided that the great intervening agency between the ex-slave and his ex-owner was to be the labor contract. It must be remembered that the idea of contract—its sanctity, enforcement, and effect—held an unparalleled place in American history at that time and for many years to come. Great judicial and legislative fantasies had been built upon it; it had been pronounced as coming direct from the Hand of God (or, at the very least, from the hands of philosopher-kings) by the greatest leaders and judges in the land.[5] It was accepted doctrine that the capacity to make a contract was a corollary to freedom. A "radical" might have substituted "the right *freely* to contract"—but here we break down in semantics. In any case, it is not surprising that Howard should have placed all the freedman's eggs in a basket called "contract"; his faith in it may seem touchingly naïve to a more cynical modern observer, but it is surely understandable.

From the first, Howard ordered his agents to "quicken the industry of the Freedmen"; they must be forced to work; but also the planter must be forced to recognize his laborer's new status and to pay for labor received.[6] There remained, however, one fly in the ointment: the question of the wage scale. If the freedman was to be forced to sign labor contracts under threat of arrest, what was to prevent his employer from dictating an unfair rate of pay? Surely equity would require that compulsion on one side must be met by compulsion on the other—that is, a fixed minimum wage. Suggestions to this effect were made to Howard, but they were rejected. While he permitted agents to make decisions of this sort on a local basis (that is, to annul or refuse to validate contracts calling for excessively low wage scales), he steadfastly refused to establish a bureau-wide policy on the matter. Bentley argues that this represented Howard's feeling that "circumstances differed so greatly between localities and among individual workers that no wage scale could be fair."[7] A more likely explanation would be the innate faith of a nineteenth-century conservative in the "American way." The doctrine of "liberty of contract" had not yet made its appearance on the American legal scene, but the groundwork for it had been laid long before the general made his decision.

I am not suggesting that the bureau and the army represented a monolith, determined to reenslave the freed slave. As shown below, both agencies tried to protect the rights of the freedmen, within certain limits. Indeed, some of their representatives used their powers to the fullest extent to destroy the emerging system of labor control. The basic contention is merely that the general thrust of official bureau and army policies was highly support-ive of that system, and, further, that there was a general consen-sus among the planter class, the "Black Code legislatures," and the federal government's agents that no other system could or should be considered.

In Mississippi one of the first orders issued by the Freedmen's Bureau was an order to the freedmen to sign labor contracts immediately or be subject to arrest as vagrants.[8] The fact that this order is specifically addressed to "the colored people of Mississippi" is seen as a rationale of sorts for the similarly di-rected codes soon to be passed by the legislature.[9] This seems an arguable proposition, however, as the legislature theoretically represented all of the people of the state while the bureau was, as its title stated, largely concerned with the freedman alone. In any case, the legislature, as we have seen, followed the bureau's lead. Upon passage of the code, General Howard ordered that no agent should enforce the section of the so-called "Act to Con-fer Civil Rights," which barred blacks from ownership (or rental) of land. It is noteworthy that Howard did not object to either the contract provisions of the act or the enticement section.

The army's response to the code was longer in coming, but more vigorous in the end. When the Mississippi authorities be-gan to use the newly passed vagrancy laws to arrest recently dis-charged black soldiers in Vicksburg, General Wood requested the mayor to give his former troops time to find employment.

Two weeks later, apparently having reached the end of his patience, Wood ordered that blacks not be prosecuted for offenses for which whites were not punished or prosecuted to the same degree. As this applied to almost all the laws of the Mississippi Black Code, he had virtually invalidated the whole structure in one stroke. One section of the Vagrancy Act, however, made no reference to color, and this law was apparently abused to its fullest extent.[10]

In South Carolina, the bureau had been in operation for some time before the passage of the codes. The army had also been forcing the blacks into labor contracts throughout 1865. It is worthy of note that the army advised straightforward service contracts, while the bureau wrote contracts that included provisions barring the laborers from leaving the plantation without the master's permission and other provisions "strongly reminiscent of slavery."[11] The passage of the Black Codes in December 1865 produced a marvelously ambivalent response. General Sickles, military commander of the Department of the Carolinas, issued a military directive nullifying the codes. Yet in that same order he commanded that his officers should create regulations to provide for "hiring out to labor, for a period not to exceed one year, all vagrants" who could not be employed on public works. Any freedmen who had not signed labor contracts within ten days were classified as vagrants.[12] The bureau's man in South Carolina showed a similar concern for planters' needs. General Scott ordered that "men or women who leave the plantation on which they are employed to labor . . . and thereby neglect their growing crops, be at once arrested as vagrants and put to work. . . . Their children, if any, will be bound to such persons as will take care of them and learn them habits of industry."[13] The legislature's acts were dead, but what planter could have asked for a better *coda* for the codes than these two directives?

In Alabama the bureau preempted the legislature by issuing labor regulations in August 1865. The standard contracts provided a laborer's lien upon the crops for wages, and bureau approval of all contracts was required. However, the contracts also included a provision that, upon the sworn statement of the employer that an employee had been absent from work without good cause for longer than one day or more than three days in any month, the employee was to be arrested as a vagrant and put to work by the county. General Swayne, head of the Alabama division of the bureau, was on "cordial terms with most of the members of the [constitutional] convention," and with the governor himself.[14] Both men tried in vain to convince the legislature that a rigorous Black Code was unnecessary. The convention's contract law was thereupon vetoed by the governor, an action for which Swayne took full credit in his letters to General Howard and reports to the bureau.[15] Neither gentleman apparently objected to the vagrancy law passed in this period, for it was signed into law, and the apprenticeship statute was specifically ordered enforced by the general, despite its preference for "former masters." The enticement statute also appears to have met with the approval of both Swayne and the governor, for it, too, became law. General Swayne was also one of the few bureau agents who felt he could rely on the justice of the civil courts in the South, and thus he did not establish bureau courts to try freedmen's cases.[16] This happy joining of forces between the bureau and state officials helped to make Alabama a favorite of President Johnson's "hatchet man," General Joseph Fullerton.

Louisiana was the scene of some of the most complicated maneuvers and conflicts over the control of the black labor force. As early as 1862, Union General Benjamin Butler had instituted a system of forced labor wherein he had turned over the black laborers to the planters. However, Butler had fixed wages, hours of labor, and working conditions.[17] When General Nathaniel Banks took over command of the Louisiana system in 1863, he continued this practice, but expanded upon it. He established a "Bureau of Free Labor," and its agents made terms between the planter and his workers. Banks continued the practice of minimum wages, but he increased the use of the "vagrancy arrest" threat to ensure that the black stayed on the plantation and did his work.[18]

When the bureau took over the task of regulating, it had as its local chief Thomas Conway, one of the more controversial figures in its history. Conway, who had been in charge of Banks's "Bureau of Free Labor," took over as assistant commissioner of the Freedmen's Bureau in 1865 and immediately established a "Department of Plantations" to handle labor affairs. With the bureau in charge of affairs, some of the army methods which had been objects of planter criticism were changed. The most significant of the changes was the elimination of a fixed wage, although agents were "encouraged" to ensure that wages did not drop below the level which slave owners had received for the hire of a slave.[19]

Despite these actions, Conway was considered a "radical" by many members of the bureau. This reputation probably arose as a result of his running dispute with Mayor Hugh Kennedy of New Orleans, who was an "unreconstructed" rebel, just pardoned by President Johnson. Kennedy was arresting as a vagrant virtually any freedman who was walking the streets of the city. Conway's view of vagrancy was on a different plane, however, and only vagabonds or drifters fell into his definition. Since he felt few of the freedmen qualified as such, he interfered with Kennedy's activities and freed civilly arrested vagrants. Further, bureau agents were ordered to enforce laborers' liens against crops.[20]

Soon Conway found himself unpopular with President Johnson, Bureau Chief General Howard, and the planter class in general. General Howard, under pressure from the president, had sent a pair of "investigators" to review the bureau's activities in the South. Having been badly burned by his original investigator, Carl Schurz, who had turned into a Radical, President Johnson wanted no further mistakes of that sort. He had, after all, personally given "his unequivocal approval" to the administration of Louisiana, and Howard was anxious to cause him no displeasure. Therefore, after a critical report from General James Fullerton, a "Johnson man" to his fingertips, Conway was unceremoniously fired. He was not even given the usual sop of a post in the Washington office of the bureau.[21] Fullerton, who later in the year was to discount all stories of southern atrocities against blacks and to advise Johnson to veto the second Freedman's Act, was acting commissioner.

In his brief tenure, Fullerton made clear that bureau agents were to permit the free market to operate with regard to wages. He felt that labor was overregulated and that this caused the freedman to become "too excited and created a distrust in his mind of planters' attitudes" and a similar distrust by the planter of the new labor system. Agents were to refrain from setting minimum wage or maximum hours scales and to permit the freedman to make his own contracts. To encourage this "free market" Fullerton openly encouraged the civil authorities to enforce the vagrancy laws, as he, unlike Conway, saw large numbers of black vagrants in the city. He closed the bureau courts, but offered to take control of convicted vagrants and put them to work in the fields. When General Absalom Baird took over the bureau from Fullerton a month later, he simply continued to build on his predecessor's framework.[22] Thus Louisiana soon found itself in the same pattern established in the states discussed above.

In Georgia the situation is perhaps best summed up by the Georgia Apprenticeship Law in the Black Codes of 1866. The legislature simply made valid under state law the contracts of apprenticeship made by agents of the Freedmen's Bureau. Assistant Commissioner Davis Tillson ordered that when freedmen refused to sign labor contracts, the bureau agents should make contracts for them, to be as binding as if made "with the full consent of the freed people."[23] While the army commander invalidated those sections of the Georgia codes which discriminated by race, the bureau issued an order which told the freedmen that unless they signed labor contracts within three days, they would be arrested as vagrants and "the chain gang will be your inevitable fate."[24]

In Virginia, the problems of "mixed rule" became clear. General Alfred Terry invalidated the vagrancy statute, which made no reference to race but was, in the general's eyes, an attempt "to reduce the freedmen to a condition of servitude worse than that from which they have been emancipated—a condition that will be slavery in all but its name."[25] However, the other two military commanders whose districts included Virginia did not follow his lead. Furthermore, bureau agents in his district were threatening to arrest idle freedmen "according to the vagrant laws of the state" and their children were to be bound out until they were twenty-one years old. At least one agent hired out such vagrants to those who wanted their labor.[26]

In Florida, Assistant Commissioner Osborn of the bureau threatened to shift unemployed blacks and their families by force from the city of Jacksonville to the plantations near Tallahassee; and while the bureau did not permit the Florida courts to whip freedmen, it did promise, by agreement with the governor, to punish all those sentenced to such penalties "at the rate of one day's hard labor for each stripe spared to the Negro's back." The author of the only recent studies of the bureau in Florida concluded that the freedman was forced by the agency to take whatever contracts the planter offered.[27]

Texas was the last state to pass a Black Code, and it appears that the bureau had performed such yeoman service in enforcing its own vagrancy and contract regulations that the state legislature could afford to be "lenient" in its own laws. Assistant Commissioner Kiddoo created and enforced his own enticement laws, and Assistant Commissioner Gregory adopted the "sworn statement of employer" clause, first used in Alabama, and arrested as vagrants all who were charged with more than one day's absence (or five days in any month).[28]

This list of activities of the bureau and the army clearly does not represent anything like a full description of their policies in the period. In a brief survey of this type, only the highlights have been touched upon.[29] At the same time, one must acknowledge that both agencies did provide a basic source of justice in other areas regarding the freedmen. They protected voting rights, demanded equal access to the courts, and sometimes intervened when white gangs attempted to hold the ex-slaves in bondage.[30] The freedman's schools and the freedman's banks were noble social experiments in nineteenth-century terms. However, if the Black Code legislatures give us any clue to the major concerns of the South regarding the freed slave, it is that the creation of a system of forced labor was their paramount interest. In this regard, the bureau and the army anticipated and encouraged the desires of the old, "unreconstructed" South.

If this is true, one is forced to reckon with the apparent contradiction posed by President Johnson's veto of the second Freedmen's Bureau bill, which would have greatly increased the powers of the agency. No clear answer to this question is possible in this study. It is possible that Johnson feared what might be done in the future. Further, in order to prove that his plan of Reconstruction was working, he had just instigated some muck-raking investigations which tried to show that the bureau had surreptitiously maltreated blacks in order to flay the South with atrocity stories. His ferrets also claimed to have discovered in-numerable cases of corruption. However, it is noteworthy that, through all of this, he never even threatened General Howard with dismissal—an act that could have been accomplished with a stroke of the pen. Furthermore, when a revised bill was finally passed over Johnson's veto, Howard indulged in a little politi-cal housekeeping and purged the relatively few radicals in the bureau.[31]

It is possible that the main cause of the bureau's historical reputation arose from Johnson's attempts to discredit it during this period. In practice, it appears that even Johnson had little trouble living with it as it actually operated.

# 3

# Reconstruction
# Legislation

*[The Negroes] voted as a group against a resolution which would
have put the convention on record as being opposed to the setting
up of [racially] separate schools.*

Vernon L. Wharton

In the "horror" history of Reconstruction, perhaps the most
vilified institutions were the "Radical-Negro-carpetbagger" legislatures. From Thomas Nast's cartoons of black buffoons and
smirking, malevolent scalawags to the Dunningites' descriptions
of ignoramuses and their evil masters enacting laws without any
idea of, or concern for, their consequences, we are given a picture of radicalism gone wild. Surely here, where the legislators
have no understanding of the economics of agriculture or the
need for "order" in employer-employee relationships, will be
found the laws that, at least for a time, destroy the peonage system set up by the codes and the Freedmen's Bureau. Clearly, the
most simplistic remedies for relief were just the sort of legislation which ought to have come from these legislatures. A minimum wage or share law, the most direct of remedies, might have
been a logical expectation. Perhaps, in view of the numerous
complaints of false bookkeeping and overcharges made in the
early years of the contract laws, some kind of formal legal review
of charges and deductions made by the planters might have
been instituted. In brief, one is led to anticipate that these "hot-
beds of radicalism" would have significantly intruded a governmental presence into the field.

It is all the more striking, therefore, to note that no such actions were taken by any Reconstruction legislature. Even in those

states where the "carpetbagger-ignorant Negro" coalition was strong, the Radical emphasis was on suffrage, desegregation, education, and the like; legislation on labor was essentially conservative, if any positive action was taken at all.

It might prove useful at this point to review the legal structures under which the ex-slaves were forced to operate at the time the Radicals took power in the congressionally reconstructed states. The freedman was forced, by bureau and army orders or by contract or vagrancy laws, to contract for his labor with a planter. He might be paid wages (with half of these withheld until the crop was harvested) or receive a share of the crop. Under sharecropping, advances made to him by the planter (usually in scrip or in goods) for food, seed, tools and housing were often evaluated by the lender. The lien concept, originally written into bureau contracts to protect the worker, became an instrument by which he was bound to the land. The planter (or merchant) who lent the goods, was given a lien on the crop. Even if the cropper were to have a crop plentiful enough to remove his overvalued debts after the harvest, he would have to borrow again to survive the winter. The wage-paying employer could fine his worker for absence from work (regardless of cause) or for failure to meet standards of performance set by the employer himself. Under pressure to sign a contract, any contract, the freedman was in no position to bargain about his wages. Should he find himself dissatisfied with his contract as it actually operated and try to leave his employment, he was often subject to arrest for breach, or for vagrancy. In any case, all his earnings (should he leave) were forfeit regardless of how much labor and time had been invested. Finally, where was the dissatisfied laborer to go? The enticement laws made it risky for anyone else to employ him, under threat of severe civil or criminal penalties, and the cost of traveling out of the region was beyond the financial capabilities of all but a few. The binding of the servant to the master was almost complete.

This is not to say that the system was totally effective in its actual operation; what system of laws ever is? The planters were constantly complaining of workers leaving, attracted by higher wage offers, the lure of the city, or simple wanderlust. The thesis that underlay the construct of laws, however, was clear, and the

evidence is that most of the freedmen worked and worked fairly
well.[1]

The story of Reconstruction legislation is a confused one. No
one seemed sure exactly which laws were in force in 1868. For
example, that portion of the Black Code of Louisiana which the
governor failed to sign, and which had never become part of the
code of laws, was nevertheless repealed by the 1869 legislature
early in the session.[2] The vast numbers of private bills passed by
these legislatures make a study of the statute records exceed-
ingly tedious and confusing; and inaccurate codification of laws
and court cases further exacerbates the confusion.[3] Understandably there is little scholarship on Reconstruction legislation by
the states, other than the "Dunningites'" concentration on corruption in financial matters and the Revisionist responses. With
this caveat in mind, let us examine the reactions of the "reconstructed" legislatures to the plight of the freedman.

The South Carolina legislature, counted among the most radical of all, made a contract law one of its first priorities. In "An
Act to protect laborers and persons working under contract on
shares of crops" they provided that "whenever such contract or
contracts are violated, or attempted to be violated or broken . . .
before the conditions of the same are fulfilled . . . complaint may
be made, before a Justice of the Peace or Magistrate or . . . any
Court having jurisdiction in such cases." Breach of contract, by
either party, was a punishable offense. However, "if the offending party be the landowner or owners" he might be punished by
a fine of "not less than fifty dollars, nor more than five hundred
dollars." On the other hand, "If the offending party be a laborer
or laborers . . . [he] shall be liable to fine or imprisonment, according to the gravity of the offense."[4] Theoretically, the fact
that the planter was subject to any punishment for breach of
contract was an advance over the provision in the Black Codes.
As a practical matter, it had little meaning, since employers were
simply not prosecuted under the statute. This is made clear by
virtually all contemporary accounts; in addition, I have read all
reported cases under the statute and no planter was ever a defendant. (N.B., not all cases are reported, but only those which
have reached the appellate courts.) The fact that simple breach

was made a crime was enough to ensure the subservience of the laborer; and the incredible disparity in punishments (with the laborer subject to the whim of the presiding justice of the peace, without limits) is clear evidence of the tenor of the statute.[5]

Furthermore, by giving jurisdiction in such cases to justices of the peace, the legislature was ensuring that the law would be enforced by those most likely to be sympathetic to the employer. The "Courts of superior jurisdiction" were seen by General Howard as places where blacks might be dealt with fairly, but he conceded that "it is notorious that he [the Negro] stands little or no chance before a jury or magistrate of inferior jurisdiction."[6]

With regard to the lien laws, the legislatures' actions were less precise. The lien system grew out of the disruption of the plantations. The farmer had to have something to pledge in order to get supplies on credit from merchants. As land was not highly valued immediately after the war, the planter pledged his ungrown, often unplanted, crop against the loan. The merchant then had a lien against the crop when it was harvested. (The Freedmen's Bureau essentially initiated the lien idea in its labor contracts by giving the worker a lien for his wages on the ungrown crop.) This system had injurious effects on all small farmers and even on some large plantation owners, but its effects fell hardest on the black cropper.[7]

The South Carolina Republican legislature's first action in this regard was a positive one. The 1866 lien laws were kept in effect, but they were amended in 1869 to give the laborer a first (or prior) lien. This meant that the laborer's claim on the crop was to be settled before the merchant's lien could be executed. This was clearly a prolabor statute, but it was not to last. In 1874, the legislature added a landlord's lien to the general statute and, most significantly, made this lien for advances prior to all others.[8]

Perhaps even more significantly, the Radical legislature enacted a statute that validated the practice of making parol (or oral) contracts between master and servant. The only contracts of this sort which could be enforced were those not exceeding one year's service, but, of course, this was precisely appropriate for agricultural matters.[9] In any case, it is doubtful whether a statute enforcing oral contracts of longer duration would have been upheld by the higher courts, because the common law tradition in South Carolina (and almost every other state) barred enforcement of parol contracts in excess of one year's service.[10]

As important as these statutes themselves were, their interpretation by the South Carolina courts was of equal import to the black worker. For example, the act of 1869 did not give a sharecropper a lien on the crop unless his contract was in writing. The landlord's lien, however, could be based on a parol contract.[11] Furthermore, the acts of 1866 and 1872 were interpreted by the courts not to give a lien to a "mere laborer for hire" nor to a "mere cropper," on the ground that the master-servant relationship does not exist in such cases.[12] It is all the more noteworthy, then, that the Supreme Court of South Carolina did find such a master-servant relationship when it came to enforcing, under common law, an action for enticement. It was necessary to use the common law remedy, said the court, because the 1865 act regulating "the domestic relations of persons of color," which did give such a remedy against enticement, had been repealed in 1872.[13] Thus the cropper was a servant, should he try to leave his employer, but a "mere laborer" should he attempt to get a lien on the crop. This seems much more a set piece of tortured reasoning than any attempt at legalistic rebuttal.

The legal strictures placed on the freedom of the black agricultural laborer in South Carolina, the state often described as the classic example of Reconstruction, where "the rule of the Radical Republicans was most prolonged," provide the soundest evidence that all parties in the South agreed on the necessity for a legalized system of labor control. The fact that the system was closer to slavery than to freedom was insufficient reason to challenge it.

Mississippi, whose Black Code was perhaps the most repressive, seems to have taken the most vigorous action to improve matters. The incredible apprenticeship and vagrancy laws, which had caused more uproar in the North than anything else, were slowly emasculated by the military governors and the legislature itself, though it was not until the Reconstruction legislature of 1870 came into power that they were fully repealed. The legislature repealed all of the sections of the code which made racial distinctions, and the vagrancy, contract, and apprenticeship laws were thereby removed from the books. The new apprenticeship statute, while obviously made colorblind, was changed more significantly than that. It required that the parents of the potential apprentice must give their consent in order for the court to bind him over.[14] This took the teeth out of the law insofar as it provided a tool to enslave black children.

At the same time, the legislature passed a new vagrancy law, which narrowed the definition of vagrancy and, most important, did not permit the hiring out of convicted vagrants who could not pay their fines.[15] Of course, any vagrancy law could be used to discriminate against any particular class through improper and prejudiced application by the courts and legal authorities. As noted earlier, the Virginia vagrancy statute, whose purpose was precisely that, was copied from the Pennsylvania statute. How the statute was actually applied in practice is difficult to determine. No cases under this law ever reached the appellate courts; thus no cases were reported. In 1872 some planters obviously felt that this law, as it stood, could provide the basis for the return of all Negroes to "public slavery." However, their pressure on the legislature to pass firmer labor control statutes indicates that this was not being done.[16]

There is evidence that in Mississippi, as in other states, there was a significant attempt to get around the lack of a contract law. The ploy was simply to charge the laborer not with simple breach, but rather with criminal fraud.[17] The cropper who accepted, let us say, advances for the purchase of seed, would be charged, if he left the employ of the planter, with receiving money under false pretenses, a statutory offense intended for use against swindlers and confidence men. The reported cases under this statute, for the period 1868–1875, deal only with apparently legitimate applications of the law; so whether or not it was perverted to punish simple breach cannot be known.[18] It is not likely, however, that a black laborer could have appealed such a conviction.

The practice of hiring out convicted felons was opposed by the legislature. The military commander in Mississippi, General A. C. Gillem, had leased all of the state's penitentiary inmates to an enterprising plantation owner and paid him some eighteen thousand dollars a year in addition.[19] But in 1872 the legislature debarred the leasing of convicts and started construction of a series of prison farms. This was so uneconomical, however, that in 1875, the last year of Republican rule, the legislature gave up and permitted the leasing of county convicts to outside contractors.[20]

The whole convict lease system presents an extraordinarily complex problem, and it will be discussed in greater detail in the next chapter. However, one important distinction should be made at this point. The leasing of penitentiary (that is, *state*) convicts involved a contract between a public authority (usually the board of commissioners of the penitentiary) and a contractor who took whole blocks of workers. County convicts, on the other hand, could in general be hired out either en masse or as individuals, sometimes by a board and sometimes by the local judge. In the latter case, the convict often made a *private* contract with his employer to work out an indebtedness caused by the employer's payment of the felon's fine and costs. While the public contract system provided both a windfall for employers and slavery of a sort for the convict, the private contract fitted a classic definition of peonage. In this case, the Mississippi Republicans permitted only public contracts by county boards of supervisors, and, in that sense, demonstrated their distaste for the latter system.[21]

The first lien law of Mississippi was passed in 1867 by the "unreconstructed" legislature. It was intended merely to provide liens for merchants based on advances to planters. But in 1872 the Radicals passed a new statute giving the laborer a lien on the crop for the first time.[22] At this point, the landlord had no lien on the crop for rents, but in a slick piece of judicial legislation, the courts gave him a lien on his laborer's share of the crops for advances made by him. In 1873 the legislature gave the landlord a lien on the crop for rent.[23] While, theoretically, the laborer still had the prior claim under the law, the courts reduced and virtually removed this priority over the years.[24] Finally, the laborer's position was made a total farce by the ruling of the courts that the laborer's lien could be waived by parol. "He may rely upon the promise of his employer for his pay, and waive his lien in favor of the mortgagee." Whether there had been such a waiver was a question of fact for the jury or the court.[25] The likelihood of a black cropper's testimony in this regard being given more weight than his employer's, particularly in a local court (whose decisions in laborer's lien cases were final) seems slim to the point of nonexistence.[26]

With the exception of this area, however, the Mississippi Radical legislature has by far the best record of any legislature in Reconstruction. While there are indications that the system of forced labor did operate to some degree at the local level, at least it did so without legal sanction.

In Alabama, where the Black Codes had been "moderate," the legislature did not repeal them. The governor had vetoed the contract law as unnecessary (because of the good works of the federal authorities), and the only laws of interest which had been enacted were the vagrancy and enticement statutes. The Vagrancy Act of 1866 was not repealed in full; it was, in fact, being enforced in the state throughout Reconstruction.[27] In the absence of a contract law, the planters did use the false pretenses ploy, occasionally succeeding.[28] The enticement law was enforced to the fullest degree, and courts consistently upheld it. It was challenged as early as 1870 on the grounds that it violated the 1866 Civil Rights Bill passed by the Congress. In *Murrell* v. *State*, the Alabama Supreme Court denied the contention on the grounds that the law had no openly discriminatory phraseology.[29] The language of the court, however, made clear that the act was intended to "operate chiefly in respect to colored agricultural laborers."[30]

The Alabama legislature acted as early as 1868 to establish convict labor laws and kept active in the area throughout Reconstruction.[31] The private contract was not instituted formally, however. The lien laws followed the predictable pattern: in 1868 the laborer was given a lien on the crop, "subordinate only to liens for rent," but by 1871, the employer had a lien "superior to all other liens" for "advances made" as well. The courts soon accepted "a verbal agreement for a lien on the crop for supplies furnished" only, despite some strictures against it in the Statute of Frauds, and the circle was closed.[32]

Louisiana also had an extended period of Republican rule, and the major provisions of the codes left standing by the bureau had already been repealed by the "unreconstructed" legislature of 1866–1868. Despite the extraordinary efforts of the

Freedmen's Bureau to force the freedman to work, the Louisiana planters were still unsatisfied. In 1867 the planters initiated a successful drive to have blacks arrested on trumped-up charges and released to them to work out their fines. Despite this obvious misuse of the law, one of the first acts of the Radical legislature was to pass a new vagrancy law almost on a par with the original Black Code provision.[33]

The enticement law was not reenacted, and the courts in 1867 had declared that "enticing away from defendant's . . . plantation, certain freedman laborers . . . [is not an] offense known to our laws."[34] The lien laws go as usual: in 1867 the laborer gets a lien for the first time; by 1870 it is inferior to that of the employer for rent and advances, and so forth as in other states.[35] On balance, the Louisiana Republicans come off pretty well.

Georgia, on the other hand, had a relatively brief period of Radical rule before the conservatives won power. There was no distinction, however, between the Radical and conservative legislatures on the subject of peonage. The Georgia enticement law, passed in 1866, was vigorously enforced. The courts applied it to verbal contracts as well as written ones and apparently applied it often. In fact the law was held to apply even if the servant in question had not yet begun his term of service and no damage could be shown.[36] The general understanding about which sort of laborers the act was dealing with is made clear by the judges' opinions. In 1906 Justice Cobb of the Georgia Supreme Court declared, while giving a history of the act, that "as the servant class in this State was made up largely of negroes, the effect of this statute was not to punish the negro who violated his contract, probably through ignorance that such an act involved any moral obliquity, but to punish the persons (generally white persons) who brought about the wrong . . . to prevent as far as possible the disastrous effects resulting from . . . servants being enticed to violate their contracts of employment."[37] The justice was undoubtedly correct about what the legislature intended, but the laborer *was* apparently being punished for violation of contract despite the lack of a contract law. For instance, when a certain planter claimed that his laborers had deserted him and "hired themselves to the agent of another" he had them arrested and jailed, under something known as the Court Contract Act.

When the laborers were released "to go to the plaintiff's plantation, but returned to that of the defendant . . . they were arrested a second time and sent to jail." This time they were released by the Freedmen's Bureau and were "returned" to the
enticer's lands.[38]

What is fascinating about the case is not the enticement statute
under which it was brought but rather the nature of the act
under which the *laborers* were originally jailed. According to
Judge Montgomery of the Georgia Supreme Court, the first
owner's "contract with the negroes was a Court contract . . . [al-
though it had never been] filed in the office of the County Court.
Assuming it to have been a Court contract, West [the plaintiff]
seems to have taken the course pointed out by the law for its
enforcement, to wit: *attachment*."[39] While the original jailing took
place in 1868, the judge was speaking in 1872, and he still could
see nothing strange about the attachment of black workers—that
is, their arrest and imprisonment. Presumably this particular
ploy was not always successful, for the Georgia courts denied a
more common method of enforcing contracts without a contract
law in *Ryan* v. *State*. Here an action was brought under *Revised
Code* 4507, a penal statute punishing "cheats and swindlers" for
receiving money under false pretenses. Again the charge was
really simple breach of contract, and the court denied the applicability of the statute, ruling that "a promise is not a pretense."[40]

Thus, although Georgia had no contract law, it seems highly
likely that many laborers were forced, under threat of penal
sanction, to fulfill labor contracts (written or unwritten). It must
be remembered that the fact that the "false pretenses" statute
was declared inapplicable in *Ryan* did not mean that it was not
used often, in cases which never reached the higher courts. In
fact, the same tack was still being used in 1886 and therefore one
gets the impression that it was widespread.[41]

Convict labor was started in Georgia by General Thomas
Ruger, military commander of the district in 1868, who leased
several hundred convicts to railroad contractors. When the Radical government came into power, one of the first acts of Governor Rufus Bulloch was to confirm the lease and to contract out
three hundred more convicts.[42] Further, the Black Code vagrancy law provided for the hiring out of convicted vagrants to

pay their fines, and this practice was apparently highly popular. The legislature passed a statute declaring that "when any person is convicted of any crime or misdemeanor, the punishment whereof . . . is fine or fine and costs . . . the convict might . . . hire himself or herself to any citizen of this state."[43] Thus Georgia supported not only the public but the private contract.

The actions of the Georgia legislature on lien laws were consistent with the now familiar progression seen in other states.[44] In sum, the situation of the black agricultural laborer in Georgia was almost a classic definition of peonage.

In North Carolina, the 1866 vagrancy law was still being enforced in 1871, although a substitute measure (with no substantial changes) had just been passed.[45] The enticement act of 1866 was also still in force, and in 1874 the North Carolina Supreme Court declared that it was valid. This was done despite the fact that the contract in question gave the employer total power "to decide as to the performance or non-performance," and provided that, if the worker "shall misbehave *in the opinion of the party of the first part* such misbehaving party shall quit the premises and *forfeit to the party of the first part*, all his interest in the common crop." The private convict labor contract was also approved in this state.[46] Otherwise, the North Carolina statutes are similar to those of other southern states.

Rather than repeat the development of these laws in an endless litany, let it be said that the states represented above are fairly typical of their sisters.[47] There are, of course, differences in approach and enforcement, but a broad and reasonably consistent pattern does emerge. By and large, even in the "Tragic Era," when Radicalism is supposed to have run rampant over the prostrate South, the newly freed agricultural worker was, by consensus, placed in a position of peonage. Sometimes, in the absence of specific laws to enforce one area of labor control or another, extralegal methods were employed, but in the main, the laws themselves (and their interpretations by the courts) provided an adequate tool for the job.

# 4
# Redemption

*The deficiencies in the historiography of the American Negro lie
mainly in the realm of omission, and nowhere is this so apparent as
in the treatment of the Negro in the years 1876–1896.*

Jack Abramowitz

In most of the histories of blacks in the South, the chapter following the discussion of Reconstruction and Reunion is almost
ineluctably entitled "The Negro Migration" or "The Negro
Moves North." In fact, the period between 1877 and the end of
the Populist movement is perhaps the least documented in all
black history. To be sure, there are always references to the Colored Farmers' Alliance in the 1880s and 1890s, but these are
wholly inadequate as a description of what was happening to the
black agricultural worker in this period. For it was at this time
that the variety of legal structures designed to keep that worker
in a state of quasi slavery were refined, strengthened, and made
part of the fabric of southern life and law. This development will
be discussed in relation to the lien laws, convict labor, and the
contract and enticement laws.

The lien laws, as we have seen, began as a method by which
the planter could get credit at a time when his land had little
value. While they were by no means a postbellum innovation,
most of them were passed either as part of the Black Codes or as
Reconstruction legislation. These first laws, it should be noted,
gave the whip hand to the merchant and not to the planter. The
first additions made by the Republicans tended to be the grant-
ing of a first lien to the laborer. The next step was the landlord's
lien, which soon became, as a pattern emerged, the prior lien on
the crop. Finally, as Reconstruction drew to a close, the worker's
lien lost its utility, either through direct legislation or judicial

emasculation. Despite these emendations, however, no one but the merchant was really content with the lien system, and it is interesting to note that the new Democratic governments in some states immediately repealed them. In South Carolina, for example, the first "Redeemed" legislature repealed the merchant's lien in its 1877 session. The Bourbons argued against the lien system on the grounds that it encouraged landless tenants to "squat on poor ridges and set themselves up as farmers." As no viable alternative to the lien laws emerged, however, the legislature reenacted them before the repealer ever took effect. As part of the same act, the landlord's privileges were expanded to cover all of the crop (the Republicans had restricted such liens to no more than one-third) and the validity of the parol contract was reaffirmed.[1] This end product was similarly produced in virtually all southern states, though not necessarily with the same chronology.

One aspect of this emerging system which has not been touched on was the introduction of the invidious "two-price" idea: the price of goods paid for in cash was far less than the price of the same goods lent on credit. The credit price, according to a contemporary reporter, "was never less than thirty percent and frequently runs up to seventy percent" higher than the cash price.[2] Further, once a lien had been executed, no one would sell goods to a farmer except for cash, since his only security was already pledged. "Free-market capitalism" had been successfully replaced by a state-supported freedom for the entrepreneur; there was to be no bargaining for a better price.

When an English creditor was accused in Parliament of usury for charging an Irish peasant 43.5 percent interest, a federal judge, speaking before the Arkansas Bar Association, asked, "What is 43.5%, compared to the profits charged by the holders of Anaconda mortgages on tenants in Arkansas? They would scorn 43.5%."[3] While Professor Woodward emphasizes the effects of the system on the planters, it should be made clear that the laws had their most deleterious effect on the cropper and the tenant. The landlord's lien had been made superior to the merchant's, and many planters got into the business of lending supplies themselves. Further, while both black and white suffered under these conditions, the white cropper had a far better chance of emerging from the morass. He received some degree of fair treatment from the courts, and the threat of prison hung far less menacingly (if at all) over his head.[4]

The growth of sharecropping and tenantry as alternatives to wage labor was a marked tendency throughout Reconstruction and increased during Redemption. Clearly, the changes in the lien laws reflected this shift and provided a means of regulating the black labor force under these new conditions. A side effect of the lien system was to bind both landlord and sharecropper almost exclusively to cotton as the main crop because of its ready convertibility to cash.[5]

Like the lien system, the leasing of convict labor got its start in the Reconstruction period. As noted above, the first leasings were initiated by various army commanders in the South. Initially, the rationale for this practice was defensible: the state penitentiaries had been destroyed, and some means of control had to be established. During Republican rule leasing was seen as a temporary expedient, to be used only until the penitentiaries had been rebuilt.[6] The efforts of the Mississippi legislature to forestall the permanent use of the system are typical of (if more vigorous than) the ambiguous behavior of the Reconstruction legislatures on the matter. As in Mississippi, financial considerations became paramount; the promise of a profit was far more alluring than the certainty of a large expenditure. At first the lease system provided only a slight reduction in cost over a straight penitentiary program. In Georgia, North Carolina, Tennessee, and Arkansas, the contractors essentially did no more than relieve the state of the burden of feeding and clothing its convicts, and in Mississippi and Florida, the contractors were actually paid for their trouble.[7]

By the early 1870s, convict leasing began to turn a profit, particularly as the southern states embarked on railroad construction and other internal improvements. Despite this, the real impetus for expansion of the system came after Reunion. There were two major contributions to this expansion. The first was the realization that the South had vast areas of unexploited natural resources which provided a real source of attraction for investors. Part of the attraction was the availability of cheap labor, and the convict lease system was the apotheosis of that. As George

Washington Cable, a bitter opponent of leasing, noted, it "holds forth the seductive spectacle of these great works, which everybody wants and no one wants to pay for, growing apace by convict labor that seems to cost nothing."[8]

Perhaps of equal importance to the expansion of the system was the fact that it dealt almost exclusively with blacks. This had been true even in Reconstruction, but it became absolutely clear in the latter part of the seventies. In 1875 the Georgia legislature, now "Redeemed," passed its "pig-law" which raised the penalty for hog-stealing from that of a misdemeanor to that of a felony "unless the jury recommend to mercy." Mississippi's first Democratic legislature passed an even more invidious act which made it a felony to steal any property in excess of ten dollars in value or any livestock whatever.[9] Georgia's penitentiary population leaped from five hundred to one thousand five hundred in the two years after the passage of the law, and in Mississippi it went from two hundred and fifty to one thousand. Up to 95 percent of these "new" convicts were black. This was no surprise to anyone, of course, and it was "understood" which sort of convicts were to be leased. George Tillman, a South Carolina planter and politician said, "The negro has a constitutional propensity to steal, and in short to violate most of the ten commandments. The State should farm out such convicts."[10] Wharton notes that there was a general feeling that white men should not be included in chain gangs, and their fines or punishments were therefore remitted by the mayor or judges. Alabama forbade the mixing of black and white convicts by contractors, though few contractors wanted white labor.[11] In general, the few whites who were actually sent to prison were charged with serious crimes, such as murder or arson, which often debarred them from work outside the prison.[12] In states where such restrictions were not applied, it was almost impossible to get a jury to send a white man to be farmed out.[13]

By the mid-1880s the convict lease system had reached its peak. Convict labor was lauded as reliable and cheap by the happy exponents of entrepreneurial liberty in the "Redeemed" South. United States Senator Joseph E. Brown, of Georgia, had a twenty-year lease guaranteeing him three hundred convicts ("able-bodied, long-term men") per year, for which he paid the state the munificent sum of seven cents per man per working day. The senator praised this sort of labor in Congress, for "no matter what goes wrong you have no labor strike." This emphasis on the reliability of convict labor was apparent to all. Even if your convicts should die, the contract called for their prompt replacement. And die they did, in fantastic numbers. In South Carolina, the death rate of convicts leased to the Greenwood and Augusta Railroad averaged 45 percent a year for a period of two years, 1877–1879.[14] This figure is the worst recorded, but state averages ranged from about 16 percent (in Mississippi) to 25 percent (in Arkansas) in this period.[15]

In 1886 the United States Commission of Labor issued a report on convict labor, and perhaps this provides the best summary of what was going on in the South. The main emphasis of the report was on the effect of convict labor in competition with free labor, a matter being given close consideration in many states. Thus the comments on the conditions of convict laborers are by way of off-hand summations, a fact which does not make them any the less revealing. In Alabama, the commissioner notes, "Convict labor more reliable and productive than free labor. Ninety percent of them negroes of low class, who are benefited by regular work. Mine owners say they could not work at a profit without the lowering effect in wages of convict-labor competition. The convict accomplishes more work than the free laborer." On the county level: "Great hardship through extension of sentences to work out court costs. Convicts frequently overtasked on farms." In Georgia, convicts were "barbarously treated . . . [and] worked to the utmost . . . the death rate is very high." In Mississippi: "Most of the convicts (ninety-two percent) are negroes of the lowest class. They are generally overworked, and the death rate is high. . . . Convicts do thirty percent more work than free laborers, being worked long, hard and steadily. . . . Convict labor more reliable." Or Tennessee: "Wretched surroundings, bad management, appalling death rate. The prison system is in all ways atrocious . . . but the state makes a large profit from the convict labor."[16]

It should be noted that many states throughout the nation had some form of convict labor system, but comments like these are reserved for the "Redeemed" South. Woodward notes that the "convict-lease system did greater violence to the moral authority of the Redeemers than did anything else. For it was upon the tradition of paternalism that the Redeemer regimes claimed authority to settle the race problem and 'deal with the negro.'"[17] There seem to be numerous other grounds upon which this "moral authority" might have been challenged, as the peonage laws discussed below demonstrate, but it is also clear that the convict labor practices were the most brutal of all the devices used to restore "order" to southern labor. It even aped the old slave system by quoting prices for classes of prisoners—"full hands," "medium hands," and so forth—with phrasing taken directly from slave terminology.[18] Despite rising opposition from the Grange and labor organizations, the system did not begin its decline until the depression of 1893, when it became difficult to find contractors with whom to place the leases.[19] Ultimately the state took control of the convicts, generally working them on the roads, but removing them from the hands of private contractors.

It should be made clear that the system referred to in the preceding pages is that of contracts by public authorities for "faceless" convicts. That is, the contractor had not hired individuals, but a mass of labor, whose parts were interchangeable. Theoretically, if a convict lived long enough (a doubtful proposition), his sentence would be served, and he would be released— to be replaced by another cog in the machine. This differs from the practice of hiring out an individual to work out his fine and costs. As we have seen, this latter method was among the most popular features of the Black Codes. Vagrancy laws were so commonly used for this purpose that the commissioner of labor omits them from his report, as being well known and "similar in their provisions."[20] Beyond this, however, eight states of the Confederacy had, by the mid-1880s, laws permitting such hiring for all misdemeanor or felony convicts sentenced to pay a fine (and costs). The only exceptions were South Carolina, Louisiana, and Alabama—and Louisiana took up the practice in 1894. Alabama permitted the extension of terms of those sentenced to hard labor by adding on court costs to be worked out; South Carolina apparently never succumbed.[21]

What this concept produced was a system by which the courts

became an employment agency for the planter. Ray Stannard Baker described this sort of operation in *Following the Color Line*.

> One of the things that I first couldn't understand in some of the courts I visited was the presence of so many white men to stand sponsor for Negroes who had committed various offenses. . . . I saw a Negro brought into court charged with stealing cotton.
>
> "Does anybody know this Negro?" asked the judge. Two white men stepped up and both said they did. The judge fined the Negro $20 and costs, and there was a real contest between the two white men as to who should pay it—and get the Negro. They argued for some minutes, but finally the judge said to the prisoner:
>
> "Who do you want to work for, George?" The Negro chose his employer and agreed to work four months to pay off his $20 fine and costs.
>
> Sometimes a man who has a debt against a Negro will sell the claim—which is practically selling the Negro—to some farmer who wants more labour.[22]

If the sentence given in this case was enforced, then this particular felon was not being treated badly, for the period of his servitude was limited. The more common practice was for the planter to subtract from the wages due to his worker the costs of food, clothing, and shelter. As the planter set the value of these items, with a little judicious bookkeeping the sentence could easily be made to run for a year or more. Just as the legislature and courts had cooperated in making the convict lease system a success, so the courts helped to make the "fine-cost" system function effectively. United States District Court Judge Emery Speer, a Georgian, and a bitter opponent of peonage, did a personal survey of the county court records of Bibb County, Georgia, for a one-month period. He found that more than 149 people (almost all black) had been sentenced to a total of nineteen years at labor for crimes no more serious than walking on the grass or spitting on the sidewalk.[23]

It was in this same period that the labor contract and enticement laws were formally adopted, broadened, or strengthened in most of the South. In 1908 Assistant Attorney General Charles Russell said: "The chief support of peonage is the peculiar system of State laws prevailing in the South, intended evidently to compel service on the part of the working-man."[24]

It should be noted that the system, peculiar though it was, had some precedents in American history. Besides the old practice of "indentured servants" which came with colonization, Richard Morris has traced similar usages in the antebellum South.[25]

In addition, the United States had acquired a formal system of peonage in 1846, when New Mexico became a territory. *Peon* is a Spanish word meaning foot soldier, but the term was used in the colonial system of forced labor applied to native workmen. When Spain debarred the use of these feudal tactics in 1811, the ruling landlords devised the system of debt slavery. This system was recognized by the United States and enforced in its courts after 1846.[26] In fact, the first antipeonage statute directly refers to the territory of New Mexico.

While New Mexican peonage is often discussed by legal scholars of the late nineteenth century, little mention is made of a similar situation which existed in Hawaii. There, under a labor control act of 1859, a laborer could be compelled to serve for the full term covered by his contract, and if he absented himself from work, he could be compelled to serve for a period not to exceed double the time of his absence. This provision was upheld in the courts, even after the passage of the Hawaiian Constitution of 1864, which prohibited involuntary servitude. Once again, the system comes into play when dealing with nonwhite laborers, in this case the native Hawaiians and the immigrant Japanese and Chinese imported by the sugar plantation owners.[27]

Despite this background, there is no indication that the peonage laws passed in the South had any but a homegrown basis. Aside from Texas and Virginia, which essentially drop from view in this regard, all the southern states had passed, strengthened, and modified contract labor laws by the turn of the century.[28] Once again, both legal authorities and antipeonage authors fail to note fully the widespread extent of these laws.[29] The Georgia act is typical; it reads:

> Sec. 1. If any person shall contract with another to perform for
> him services, with intent to procure money or other thing of value

thereby, and not perform the service contracted for, to the loss and damage of the hirer; or, after having so contracted, shall procure from the hirer money or other thing of value, with intent not to perform such service, to the loss and damage of the hirer,—he shall be deemed a common cheat and swindler.

Sec. 2. It is provided that satisfactory proof of the contract, the procuring thereon of money or other thing of value, the failure to perform the services so contracted for, or failure to return the money so advanced with interest thereon, at the time said labor was to be performed, without good and sufficient cause, and loss or damage to the hirer, shall be presumptive evidence of fradulent intent.[30]

It should be noted that the avowed purpose of this law is "not to enforce the contract, but to punish the fraudulent procurement of money or other thing of value."[31] "The fraudulent act of the promisor in procuring money on his contract to perform services does more than create a debt. It also constitutes a crime; and the purpose of the act is not to create a remedy for the collection of a debt, but to provide punishment for the fraud."[32] It was on this ground alone that the Georgia Supreme Court upheld this law. In general, the courts conceded that the effect of the act was to enforce the contract, but they maintained that this was merely a side effect. In fact, since enforcement of the contract was not significant, a conviction could be had even if the contract itself were not civilly valid.[33] This law was upheld against a claim that it denied the equal protection of the laws, insofar as it provided for punishment for the laborer while affording the employer "absolute immunity from prosecution or punishment by reason of any infraction of said contractual obligations." Since, "in the nature of things the master does not ordinarily procure advances from his servant . . . legitimate classification is not unjust discrimination." It is, said the court, not "criminal for a child to abandon its father," but "the abandonment of a child by its father is made a misdemeanor."[34] Where penalties *are* provided for the employer as well as for his employee, however, they must be the same. The case establishing this, in South Carolina, represents the sole instance uncovered in my research in which a contract law was declared unconstitutional by a state court before federal court activity in the area got started in the early 1900s. Even here, however, the legislature had amended the act some weeks before and had equalized the penalties. Whether they "got the word" from the court beforehand is, like the action of the court itself, a moot point. The court's stand did not prevent the laborer from going to jail; it was merely declaratory in effect—a warning, as it were, not to reenact the old provisions.[35] As employers were never prosecuted in any case, it was hardly a courageous judicial blow to the system.

Georgia, which came late into the field, provides the greatest number of judicial defenses of the contract laws (and also reports decisions of the appellate courts as well as those of the Supreme Court), but the cases reported in the other states provide roughly similar rationales.[36]

This interpretation (punishing fraud rather than breach), is absolutely vital to the validity of these laws, for every state had a provision in its constitution barring imprisonment for debt. Even in the absence of federal intervention the state courts would have had to deny the validity of the contract laws if they had been forced to view them as enforcing labor contracts. As it was, they worked perfectly. It was in the nature of things that a cropper must get some sort of advance in order to raise his crop, and, once having done so, he could not leave his employer regardless of the amount of labor he had put in on that crop. Further, the provisions which delineate the nature of proof required to show fraudulent intent are highly significant. Failure to perform the services contracted for was presumptive evidence of fraud.[37]

In response to the charge that these laws constituted peonage or involuntary servitude, the courts were equally adamant. Essentially the argument ran thus: the employer under these statutes was not able to prevent his employee from leaving his employ. Neither could the courts: all that could be done was to punish him for doing so. The Supreme Court of South Carolina was "unable to discover any feature of 'involuntary servitude' in the matter. Everyone who undertakes to serve another in any capacity parts for a time with that absolute liberty which it is claimed that the constitution secures to us all, but, as he does this voluntarily, it cannot be said that he is deprived of any of his constitutional rights; and if he violates his undertaking, he thereby, of his own accord, subjects himself to such punishment as the law-making power may have seen fit to impose for such violation."[38] This assessment ignored the fact that the statute provided that imprisonment did not relieve the debt; punishment could continue indefinitely until the contract provisions had been met.

After the brief flurry of federal activity in this area, some other defenses for these laws surfaced; they will be dealt with in a later section.

The enticement laws, which made it virtually impossible for a laborer to leave his employer, also came to their full fruition by the end of the nineteenth century. All nine of the states referred to above had laws of this type on their books. Some, like Alabama, had had them since Reconstruction; others came later into the field but all had them.[39] The Florida law is fairly typical, though rather more concise than most: "Whoever shall entice, or persuade by any means whatsoever any tenant, servant or laborer, under contract with another, whether written or verbal, to violate such contract, or shall employ any servant or laborer, knowing him or her to be under contract as aforesaid, shall be punished by imprisonment not exceeding sixty days, or by fine not exceeding one hundred dollars."[40]

The effect of such a statute on the labor market is obvious, and there is less judicial coyness about the intent of these laws than about contract legislation. The Georgia courts said openly in 1871 that the legislation was intended to prevent "the derangement of an entire system of labor" and was still reiterating this line in 1907.[41] Such laws were necessary, "the servant class being largely made up of negroes." It was clearly intended to apply principally to farm laborers and was so enforced.[42] The North Carolina statute takes some of its wording directly from that portion of the Fugitive Slave Law of 1793 relating to harboring or concealing a slave, for which term "servant" is substituted.

It is highly significant that verbal contracts come under the aegis of these acts (only Alabama and Georgia required a written contract—and in Georgia this was required only if the alleged offense took place before the term of the contract began). United States Senator Thomas E. Miller of South Carolina described their effect in 1891: "In my State, if the employer states verbally that the unpaid laborer of his plantation contracted to work for the year, no other farmer dares employ the man if he attempts to break the contract rather than work for nothing: for down there it is a misdemeanor to do so, the penalty is heavy, and the farmer who employs the unpaid starving laborer of his neighbor is the victim of the court."[43]

The standards of proof required by these statutes are equally interesting. In Alabama, if a servant or laborer is "found in the service or employment of another before the termination of such contract, that fact is *prima facie* evidence . . . of a violation of that section." Further, the rule laid down in *Bryan* v. *State*, that knowledge of the previous subsisting contract was not essential to conviction, was apparently still in force.[44] Other states did not go so far, but the only safe defense against such a charge was to acquire the written consent of the former master, or to be willing to fire your employee immediately upon being informed of his previous contract.

These laws were held constitutional by the courts, against charges that they were indirect attempts to enforce contracts, and that they were class legislation.[45] It should also be noted that the fact that the servant in question had abandoned his contract before his hiring by the second employer did not absolve the latter.[46] The statutes were not simply instruments to prevent the enticement of labor; they were also intended to "constrain laborers and tenants . . . to performance of their contracts by rendering it difficult for them to secure employment elsewhere."[47]

Despite protestations that peonage was not a bascially southern practice (see, for example, Justice Jackson's opinion in *Pollock* v. *Williams*), the plain fact of the matter is that criminal punishment for breach of contract and labor enticement are found exclusively on the statute books of the southern states.[48] Kentucky, a former slave-holding state though not a member of the Confederacy, had an enticement law on its books, which had been enacted "soon after slavery ceased to exist in this state." Minnesota and Michigan had laws which punished breach with intent to defraud, after "receiving transportation from any point in this state to . . . a place where he has agreed . . . to perform labor."[49] Both of these laws were dead letters, however, and there is no record of any case being brought under them. Justice Jackson, southern apologists, and left-wing propagandists notwithstanding, peonage was both sectional and racial.[50] The South did not have what C. Vann Woodward called "the heritage of a manumitted slave psychology"; it had a metamorphosized slave psychology.[51] It had simply adapted its laws to meet the formal strictures of the Civil War amendments, in order to retain as much of its old rules of labor control as possible.

A peripheral comment should be made here about the role of the Populists in this context. The southern Populist movement has been described as "the most promising experiment in interracial cooperation . . . in the history of the South."[52] Richard Hofstadter, who excoriates the Populists, still feels constrained to note that some Populist leaders "attempted something profoundly radical and humane" in dealing with the racial question. To a degree, this sort of statement seems to be drawn from the arguments made by Woodward in his various studies of this period. However, these views ignore his own caveat in *Origins of the New South* that the gains in racial cooperation "were limited and that their significance could easily be exaggerated." Having given his warning, however, Woodward proceeds to mute it. He lauds the attempts of Tom Watson to emphasize the communality of economic interests among the races and points to the Populist rhetoric on black suffrage. "In their platforms Southern Populists denounced lynch law and the convict lease and called for defense of the Negro's political rights."[53]

What is most striking about this attitude, however, is Woodward's lack of interest in the real problems the black worker faced. He was certainly aware of the incongruity of the situation, for he notes, "It is undoubtedly true that the Populist ideology was dominantly that of the landowning farmer, who was, in many cases, the exploiter of landless tenant labor." However, "the lives of the overwhelming majority of Negroes were still [as before Emancipation] circumscribed by the farm and the plantation. The same was true of the white people, but the Negroes, with few exceptions, were farmers without land."[54]

As the emphasis in the Populist program was on the needs of property-owning farmers whose interests were threatened by eastern capital, little attention was given to the needs of agrarians who were caught in the trap of sharecropping or wage labor. This was, of course, precisely the position of the bulk of black farmers. It was largely irrelevant how the Populists reacted to, or cooperated with, the Negro granges and alliances, for these organizations did not, in any case, represent the mass of the black population of the South.

If we are to be shown real evidence of a communality of interests between black and white farmers in the Populist movement, then we need some proof of Populist opposition to labor contract laws, enticement laws, and the rest. If such evidence exists, it is not easily uncovered in Populist writings or rhetoric. In fact, when the Colored Farmers' Alliance proposed a strike of black cotton-pickers (to raise the wage to fifty cents a hundred pounds), the *Progressive Farmer*, a white Populist paper advised farmers to "leave their cotton in the field rather than pay fifty cents per hundred to have it picked." This (in the paper's eyes) was a blatant attempt by blacks "to better their condition at the expense of their white brethren."[55] Even with regard to the lien laws, the main thrust of Populist criticism was aimed at the merchant's lien, not the landlord's.

There was one area of real concern to blacks upon which the Populists did take a firm stand. This was the subject of convict leasing. However, on this issue there was a clear merging of black and white interests. Blacks were most often the direct victims of the system, but whites were put in difficulty by the competition. The labor movement was equally opposed to the system. In North Carolina the "Penitentiary has been forced to give up shoemaking, as laboring people refuse to buy convict-made shoes." Also, "The brick making industry around Atlanta . . . has been broken up almost entirely by convict-labor competition." In short, there was "strong popular feeling against [the] competitive employment of convict labor," and it was the competitive aspect that was paramount.[56] One searches in vain for similar Populist rhetoric against the short-term hiring out of individuals for nonpayment of fines.

Whatever credit the Populists deserve in regard to Negro rights lies in their sporadic support for equality of suffrage and the right to serve on juries, and in their integration efforts—including, at times, partially integrated alliance conferences.[57]

That these actions required great courage may be seen in the vicious attacks made on the Populists in the 1892 election campaign. Their subsequent retreat in this area, however, was probably as much due to the racist elements in their own core as to the political liabilities. In the end, while still seeking black support, they acceded fully to the idea of white supremacy.

Most important, the great agrarian revolt did not focus upon the problems affecting the bulk of black agrarian labor. To assume that the black peon could be concerned with, for instance, currency reform and free silver, was an absurdity. As Paul Lawrence Dunbar (a patent realist who once said "the only good thing a 'possum ever did was fill someone's belly") was to write, the Populist position on currency reform was a matter of indifference to the Negro; the issue was not what kind of money there was, but the fact that the Negro most often had no money of any kind.[58]

# 5

# Peonage and
# the Constitution

*. . . chained to an ever-turning wheel of servitude.*
U.S. *v.* Reynolds *(1914)*

It is striking that in a discussion of peonage covering a period of almost forty years no mention has been made of the role of the United States Courts, federal prosecutors, or even, except in passing, the Constitution of the United States. This is not an oversight, for the plain fact is that, after the federal participation in overturning the Black Codes, the United States government does not play any role at all in subsequent developments.[1] The reasons for this are, of course, beyond proof. The only conjecture I can propose is the same as that presented in the earlier sections on the Reconstruction period: namely, that the general consensus of all parties was that a system of control over the labor of blacks was necessary. The federal authorities, during Reconstruction, enforced such a system, and the Reconstruction legislatures either supported it or silently acquiesced in it. After Reunion, the southern black was left to the tender mercies of the Redeemers by a passive North. In any case, nothing was done.

This is not to indicate that there were no possibilities for action. The Constitution provided, in Justice Jackson's felicitous phrase, both "a sword and a shield." The "shield" is obvious: the state laws enforcing peonage (contract, enticement, private convict leasing, etc.) could have been challenged in the courts. If the laws had been found to be unconstitutional, they could no longer have provided the legal base for the system. What the decision of a Supreme Court which acted as it did in such cases as *U.S.* v. *Cruikshank*, the *Civil Rights Cases*, and *U.S.* v. *Harris* would have been is questionable, but it never got the opportunity to render one.[2] Again, the reason for this is unclear, but the cost of such an appeal, when the victim of the act in question is by the nature of the charge in debt, gives us a reasonable clue. Few cases of this sort were ever appealed to the higher state courts. Only a concerted effort by the federal government could have provided a path for such appeals. In the face of federal indifference to the matter, nothing of the sort occurred.

There was, however, also a "sword" in the hands of the attorney-general, which provided a tool for the prosecution of those who kept the black laborer in bondage. While other statutes came into use at a later date (see chapter 7), the basic statute available after the war was an "Act to abolish and forever prohibit the System of Peonage in the Territory of New Mexico, and other Parts of the United States." This bill had been passed by Congress in 1867 and, as the title suggests, was basically aimed at the system of peonage that had been inherited from the days of Spanish rule in New Mexico Territory. However, as written, it had force anywhere in the United States.[3] The operative section of the act read as follows:

> That the holding of any person to service or labor under the system known as peonage is hereby declared to be unlawful, and the same is hereby abolished and forever prohibited in the Territory of New Mexico, or in any other Territory or State of the United States; and all acts, laws, resolutions, orders, regulations, or usages of the Territory of New Mexico, or of any other Territory or State of the United States, which have heretofore established, maintained or enforced, or by virtue of which any attempt shall hereafter be made to establish, maintain, or enforce, directly or indirectly, the voluntary or involuntary service or labor of any persons as peons, in liquidation of any debt or obligation, or otherwise, be, and the same are hereby, declared null and void; and any person or persons who shall hold, arrest, or return, or cause to be held, arrested, or returned, or in any manner aid in the arrest or return of any person or persons to a condition of peonage, shall, upon conviction, be punished by fine not less than one thousand nor more than five thousand dollars, or by imprisonment not less than one nor more than five years, or both, at the discretion of the court.[4]

Clearly, this provision could have served as the basis for federal prosecution in peonage cases; it is unfortunate that it was a dead letter at the time that the system was developed. What the consequences might have been, had vigorous prosecution taken place in those formative years, is an open question, but one is led to suspect they might have been formidable. It is always easier to stop a practice before it has become entrenched by custom and social acceptance; the difficulty of doing so afterwards is clearly exemplified in the impotence of the whole array of the federal legal machinery in the area of peonage.

At the beginning of the twentieth century, however, the federal government did begin to take an interest in the plight of the southern peon. The reasons for this sudden interest are lost in time, but a variety of suggestions have been put forward. First, the president of the United States was a Republican, and it was argued that his party had a vested interest in anything that would embarrass the Democratic South. (There had, of course, been Republican presidents before—a long line of them—but the charge *was* made.) In addition, the Progressive Movement was in full cry, and the evil of peonage was just the sort of subject which had an almost universal appeal to that nebulous and vaguely identifiable body of reformers. Ray Stannard Baker, a leading Progressive journalist, was writing articles on the subject (later to be collected in a highly popular book), and there was much agitation over lynchings of blacks in the South. Southern Progressives were also touched by the subject and began some quiet activities of their own. Finally, the wave of immigration to the United States had produced a new situation—*whites* were being made peons. Indeed, the assistant attorney general's *Report on Peonage*, published in 1908, deals largely with cases involving immigrant laborers (mostly Jews). The Senate took up the cudgels in favor of the immigrants and initiated a study by the United States Immigration Commission. It is noteworthy that Assistant Attorney General Relative to Peonage Matters Charles W. Russell thought it appropriate to argue, "As I have already suggested, whether constitutional or not, and whether originally intended to be used as they are, these laws have become a trap for the enslavement of white workmen as well as black, and ought to be repealed, or amended with that fact in view. Some of them are considered to have been passed to force negro laborers to work; but if so, they are now affecting other persons, and the States formerly depending upon negro laborers exclusively need twice as many hands, and are resorting to every means to obtain them from Europe, directly or indirectly."[5] In the absence of any compelling evidence to the contrary, one is led to conclude that it was the horrendous idea of white peonage which provided the final spur to federal interest in the area.

Whatever the motivation, suddenly the peonage laws and practices of the South were under attack. The first attempt (which was something of a nonstarter) had already taken place in 1899, before the main thrust of federal action was under way. In that case, the United States district court judge examined the system of peonage as it existed in New Mexico and said that "no such system as this ever existed in Georgia. There could not be, therefore, in Georgia any such thing as holding persons under the system of peonage." He seemed shocked that such a suggestion should have been made and declared that it would be a "perversion of this act to apply it to an ordinary restraint of personal liberty."[6] As this case was not reported until many years later, however, it was not considered as a precedent in the interpretation of the act. In fact, the federal officials in the early 1900s felt they were breaking new ground.

The leading light of the early antipeonage actions of the federal government was a pronounced anti-Populist, United States Judge Thomas G. Jones. A former governor of Alabama, who had beaten the Populist candidate in an election rife with charges of fraud (he had swept the Black Belt counties), Jones was a true patrician. In the debates in the Alabama suffrage convention, he described his attitude towards blacks through an anecdote. It seems Robert E. Lee was once asked why he took such interest in the well-being of an apparently worthless soldier. Lee replied that he did so "because he is under me." "The Negro race is under us," said Jones. "He is in our power. We are his custodians . . . we should extend to him, as far as possible, all the civil rights that will fit him to be a decent and self-respecting, law-abiding and intelligent citizen. . . . If we do not lift them up, they will drag us down."[7] In true Progressive (as opposed to Populist) tradition, Judge Jones combined his patronizing attitude with a sincere respect for the use of the law and the government to solve social ills. Following his instincts, he requested that agents of the United States Secret Service investigate and report on the extent of peonage in the district. This report caused the United States district attorney for the area to bemoan the situation and state that he had "lived in this state my entire life of thirty-seven years and I never comprehended until now the extent of the present method of slavery through this peonage system."[8]

In 1903 Judge Jones empaneled a grand jury, and in a striking charge, he defined the meaning of the law. After outlining the history of the New Mexican brand of peonage, he placed the Alabama system on a par with it. Voluntary contracts are valid only as long as they remain voluntary, and the moment one party tries to "withdraw, and then is coerced to remain and perform service against his will," the servitude has become peonage. Jones pointed out that the basic requirement was that the compulsion be based on debt. It did not matter, however, whether a contract was made in consideration of a preexisting debt or a loan made at the time of the contract. The fact that a debtor might have signed a contract agreeing to such compulsion did not affect the legality of the actions, nor did the fact that the compulsion was not direct physical force but the use of the threat of law. Jones ruled that in cases of false accusation of crime (a common practice) where the accused laborer was told by an employer that his only escape from prosecution was through entering into a service contract, both the employer and the participating judge were liable. However, he did uphold as legal the practice of "confessing judgment," by which a defendant pleaded guilty and entered into a contract to pay his fine and costs.[9]

Jones also laid down rules of proof for the jury. He rejected the "reasonable man" rule. (Would the force or threats used by the employer be sufficient to constitute coercion of a reasonable man under similar conditions?) Instead, in good patrician style, the judge reminded the jury that, "as all persons are not of like courage and firmness, the court or jury . . . must consider the situation of the parties, the relative inferiority or inequality between the person contracting to perform service and the person . . . [compelling] performance, and determine in view of all the circumstances whether the service was voluntary."[10] Jones was obviously afraid that the "reasonable man" test would prevent convictions in cases where patently absurd threats of prosecution had convinced blacks, ignorant of the true nature of the law, to sign or fulfill contracts. He also noted that the "custom and habits" of a locality could not be used as a defense for offenders.

As a conclusion to this impressive performance, the judge declared one of the several Alabama peonage laws (a combination contract-enticement act) unconstitutional. "The laborer or renter who once enters into a contract and breaches it, no matter how righteously, subjects himself during the whole term of the contract to risk of prosecution if he takes like employment with others . . . [and this] impedes his right to work. . . . The law provides no means for determining the justice of his excuse, at any time, in any mode, in any tribunal, unless he first risks the penalty of hard labor. . . . *This is not required of any other freeman in the land, or exacted from any other debtor.* It is a penalty imposed for debt."[11]

As a result of all of this, the grand jury found a large number of indictments, and "some convictions were had" (four persons were convicted, one pleaded guilty).[12] Although Jones had provided an admirable start in the interpretation of the act, his ruling did not have any immediate or significantly widespread effect. This probably related to the fact that an early Florida case, *United States v. Clyatt*, which had been tried in 1902, was shortly to be decided by the United States Supreme Court. The government apparently was hesitant to push its prosecutions until that tribunal had ruled.[13]

The case of *Clyatt v. United States* was argued before the Supreme Court in December 1904. Clyatt had been convicted of "returning to peonage" two black laborers, whom he had accused of being in debt to him.[14] The basic defense consisted of three main points. First, Clyatt argued that the statute was intended to apply specifically to the system of peonage as it had existed in New Mexico. The history of the statute was traced, and great emphasis was put on the fact that the second part of the act had been directed specifically at "all persons in the military and civil service in the Territory of New Mexico."[15] The second point was related to this same section: namely, that it was *only* in the territory of New Mexico that the act could apply to individual action, not supported by state law. If the state did not support the individual actions through an authorizing statute, there could be no federal charge—this was "private action." (This idea had, of course, been successfully used in the evisceration of the civil rights bills passed by Congress during Reconstruction, on the grounds that the Fourteenth Amendment did not reach "private action."[16] Finally, Clyatt argued that there was no evidence that the laborers in the case had, in fact, been "*returned* to" peonage. All that had been proved was an unlawful arrest, an act with which Clyatt had not been charged.

In March of 1905, Justice Brewer handed down the majority decision of the Supreme Court, and the defenders of peonage had won a Pyrrhic victory. Brewer denied that the act was limited in its extent; it operates "wherever the sovereignty of the United States extends." There was no distinction between voluntary and involuntary peonage, as "this implies simply a difference in the mode of origin, but none in the character of the servitude . . . but peonage, however created is . . . involuntary servitude." The difference between peonage and free labor lies in the fact that "in the latter case the debtor, though contracting to pay his indebtedness by labor or service . . . and [although] subject . . . to an action for damages for breach of that contract, can elect at any time to break it, and no law or force compels performance or continuance of that service."[17]

Brewer dismisses the second argument of the appellant by taking a remarkably Harlan-like position on the reach of the Thirteenth Amendment, which had,

by expressly empowering Congress to enforce by appropriate legislation the prohibition against slavery and involuntary servitude, created an exception to the general rule, that the ordinary relations of individual to individual are subject to the control of the states. . . . It is not open to doubt that Congress may enforce the Thirteenth Amendment by direct legislation . . . [and] in the exercise of that power Congress has enacted these sections denouncing peonage. . . . We entertain no doubt of the validity of this legislation, or of its applicability to the case of any person holding another in a state of peonage, and this *whether there be municipal ordinance or state law sanctioning such holding. It operates directly on every citizen of the Republic*, wherever his residence may be.[18]

Significantly, Brewer pointed out that "the basal fact of peonage" is debt.[19] Debt is the cord that binds the servant to his master, and without this factor there is no peonage. This rule was to have serious implications for the future, but was not viewed as significantly weakening the government's position at the time.[20] He then went on to clarify the meaning of the terms "holding, arresting and returning": if a laborer was held in peonage, arrested with the intention of placing him in peonage or returned to peonage after having escaped from such condition, the law was violated. Having said this, however, Brewer then ruled that no evidence had been introduced to show that the laborers in question had ever previously been in bondage. If Clyatt had been charged with "arresting," the Court agreed that the conviction would have been upheld. However, as presented, the indictment was faulty, and the conviction was reversed.

As might have been expected, Justice Harlan, never a man for indulging in technicalities, dissented vigorously. He argued that the accused had not objected to having the case sent to the jury (the point at which objections to the charge would ordinarily be raised), and essentially charged his colleagues with nit-picking "in a case like this, disclosing barbarities of the worst kind against these negroes."[21]

Although Clyatt went free (the two laborers whose testimony was the basis for the government's case mysteriously disappeared and were never heard of again), the government had made its case.[22] The constitutionality of the act was established and its extent and meaning clarified. The prosecution of cases held in abeyance could now proceed apace. Indeed, for the defenders of the system, it appeared that "one more such victory and I am undone."

Between 1905 and the landmark case of *Bailey* v. *Alabama* in 1911, the Anti-Peonage Act was further defined and explicated in a variety of prosecutions at the District Court level.[23] In essence, the act was held to apply in all of the following cases:

1. Whenever a debtor is held to perform service by coercion, whether that coercion consists of the threat of violence or of prosecution under "some apparent, but void, provision of law"[24]
2. Whenever an employer falsely pretends that another is guilty of a crime and offers to bribe a prosecutor or judge in order to induce a laborer to enter into a contract to reimburse the sum paid (or allegedly paid)[25]
3. Whenever an employer causes a servant to be arrested on a warrant procured "directly or indirectly by him," and "after incarceration of the servant, should go to the jail and procure his release after he had promised to return to the employment of the master to . . . work out a debt"[26]
4. Whenever an employer falsely, or otherwise, accuses a laborer of crime in order that he may be convicted and either sentenced to hard labor in the accuser's service, or fined and forced to work out his fine in the accuser's service[27]
5. Whenever a magistrate or police official is knowingly involved in an arrest or conviction for the purpose of returning or placing the accused in a condition of peonage.[28] The act applies even if the officials in question are operating under a state or municipal law, and there is no sanctuary in their official status.[29]

As a counterpoint, the act did not apply where the fear of coercion was self-engendered, or where a magistrate or police official did not have "guilty knowledge of the unlawful purpose of the arrest."[30]

Jones's discussion of the requirements of proof was also reinforced. Justice Swayne, in his charge to a grand jury, said:

> Many artful methods for evading the effect of this statute have been devised, but none of them will avail if the juries of this country will discharge their duties fearlessly and impartially. Where it

is found that a few hours after the servant is safely lodged in jail, the master appears and proceeds to detail to him the severe results of the prosecution pending against him, and his willingness to help him out of his difficulty if he will return to work, producing on the mind of the servant a condition which leaves him no choice but to return to his employment, the master is guilty of the crime. . . . You must regard all the conditions and circumstances surrounding the cases, and determine what the motive of the prosecution was, whether or not the master directly or indirectly caused or procured the arrest, and whether the legal proceedings were taken for the purpose of creating a condition of mind in the servant whereby little or no choice was left to him in returning to the employment . . . it makes little difference what outward form the proceedings may take, if the intention of the master is illegal.[31]

Thus, with one Supreme Court ruling, and a variety of district court decisions, the initial push of the federal government on peonage was well under way.

The first reactions of the state courts to this attack on the constitutionality of their labor laws were protective ones. The defense rested on a number of legal arguments. First, some of the states defended the contract laws as simple punishments for fraud. They denied that their purpose was punishment for breach and, as noted earlier, simply argued that the state had a clear right to punish swindlers and cheats.[32] However, this was not the only arrow in the quiver.

Another standard defense lay in the fact that many states outside the South had laws on the books which punished "any person who breaks a contract of labor, having reasonable cause to believe that the probable consequence of doing so will be to endanger human life, cause grievous bodily injury, or expose valuable property to destruction." Although these statutes were intended to apply specifically to railroad switchmen and signalmen, drawbridge operators, and the like, they were cited by the courts in the South to defend their agricultural contract laws.[33] Legal experts had often defended the concept that "in the public interest, the violation of a contract may, in exceptional cases be punished." The courts now declared the violation of agricultural contracts to be an "extreme case" and therefore punishable.[34]

This concept had also been recognized in dicta in *Clyatt*.[35] The dissenting opinion in *Ex parte Hollman* states the position clearly:

> A very prevalent form of labor contract is the share system, in which the landowner furnishes land, stock, tools, seed and fertilizers, in whole or in part, and the laborer undertakes to supply all the necessary labor, for which he is to receive an agreed portion ... of the crop. ... When the busy work time on the farm arrives, the laborer is generally in debt to the landowner for advances secured. ... It is then that the dishonest laborer repudiates his obligation, and not only fraudulently deprives the owner of his property, but frequently brings disaster on the landowner's farming business. ... The utter futility of mere civil remedies ... and the necessity for some remedy, no doubt prompted the act in question.[36]

Justice Jones in his charge to the grand jury had dealt with this subject admirably in 1903:

> Surely a train dispatcher, indicted for suddenly leaving the service without giving orders necessary to prevent the clash of opposing trains upon a railroad, could not successfully plead, when destruction of life and property were brought about by his sudden leaving, that he could not be punished, because he did no more than breach a contract of service. In these and like cases, the criminal law would be exerted not to compel performance, or to prevent quitting the service in a reasonable way, but because, by abandoning it in an unreasonable way, the employee has created a condition of affairs, the natural, direct and known result of which is to endanger life, health or limb, or to inflict grievous public injury. This act [the labor act in question] is not planned with any such purpose.[37]

The final weapon upon which the state courts relied in these arguments supporting the laws, was to be found in a Supreme Court decision in 1897, revolving around the rights of seamen.[38] As far back as 1790, statutes had entitled the master of a ship to procure a warrant for the arrest of any deserting seaman, and had provided for the imprisonment of such men for breach of contract.[39] These provisions of federal law (and the foreign treaties which provided for reciprocal assistance in such cases) were challenged as unconstitutionally permitting involuntary servitude, prohibited by the Thirteenth Amendment. Justice Henry Billings Brown upheld the law, stating that the "epithet 'involuntary' does [not] attach to the word servitude continuously . . . [but only] at the inception of the servitude." The "involuntary servitude" referred to in the amendment was intended to be applicable only to "Mexican peonage and the Chinese coolie trade" and "was not intended to introduce any novel doctrine with respect to certain descriptions of servitude which have always been treated as exceptional," such as military service or apprenticeship.[40]

Brown's first point—that only servitude which was involuntary at its inception was barred—was clearly faulty, and had it prevailed no prosecutions for peonage could have taken place. The point was not essential to the decision, however, which could rest upon the "exceptional" nature of the employment. Even here Justice Harlan, whose service in defense of the broadest possible interpretation of the Civil War amendments was famous, dissented thunderously. If this interpretation were to prevail, he stormed, "we may now look for advertisements, not for runaway servants as in the days of slavery, but for runaway seamen." The Court, he said, had added an exception to the amendment by "judicial legislation" which defeated the expressed will of Congress. To do so in a case "relating to the liberty of man" was reminiscent of "monarchical and despotic governments." (Of course, the contract and enticement laws then being enforced were still productive of such advertisements "as in the days of slavery.") The dissent seemed to carry more weight than the majority opinion, for within a year the law was amended to apply only to desertion in foreign ports.[41]

In any case, the state courts continued to uphold the contract and enticement laws as valid exercises of state power. In Alabama, Georgia, and Mississippi, particularly, the courts turned down appeal after appeal.[42] In South Carolina, however, after the contract statute was declared unconstitutional by a federal court, it took only one year for the state courts to agree.[43] Perhaps more significantly, the attempts at evading the federal court rulings began to get more sophisticated. Florida, immediately after the *Clyatt* decision had come down, amended its contract law. Although the state law had not been specifically discussed in that case, the legislators could see which way the wind was blowing. Therefore, they reduced the penalties for contract violation from one thousand dollars to five hundred dollars in fines, and the imprisonment from one year to six months.[44] It is, of course, possible that a sudden surge of sympathy for the victims of the law had emerged in the legislature. On the other hand, the lower fines and penal terms put all such cases in the county judges' courts, where there was no requirement that the presiding justice have any legal training whatsoever. (Under the previous statute, the case had to be tried in a court demanding a minimum of a legal degree as a qualification for the presiding judge.) Thus, a possible declaration of unconstitutionality might have little effect upon the laymen enforcing the law.

With the exception of the South Carolina case cited above and a similar action upon one of the numerous Alabama statutes, no other declarations of unconstitutionality were made by any state court of the South before 1911.[45] Even in those cases, the declarations followed similar statements by the lower federal courts. In short, while the federal government was wielding its "sword" to some effect, the "shield" was not being equally used.

The classic test of the contract labor law took place in 1911, when the United States Supreme Court handed down its opinion in *Bailey* v. *Alabama*.[46] Oddly enough, the case did not essentially hinge upon the question of peonage, but rather on a presumptive evidence clause and a corollary rule of evidence. What had happened was fairly clear: the highest appellate courts in the South had been laying down relatively strict rules of proof in those cases where conviction under the "false pretenses" contract laws had been appealed. The contracts had to be explicit: that is, "implied contracts" were not sufficient for prosecution, and the terms of the contract (pay, length of service, etc.) had to be spelled out.[47] This requirement may seem irrelevant when one considers that oral contracts were legally enforceable in many states, but the fact was that generally no one bothered to introduce evidence demonstrating the specificity of the contract at the trials. (This is probably understandable, since convictions seemed easy to get, and few cases were appealed.)

It appears that while the higher courts would not declare the acts in question unconstitutional, they often found a technical reason for overturning cases that reached them on appeal. As the individuals who were capable of making such appeals were usually white, this did not seem to alter the system as it affected blacks. Be that as it may, the state legislatures responded by adding a new fillip to the contract laws. This was simply to add a proviso to the acts, making failure to complete the contract or refund the advance (without regard to the extent of labor performed) "*prima facie* evidence of the intent to injure or defraud."[48] Addenda of this sort (see the Georgia act quoted in chapter 4, note 30) were adopted by many of the southern states.[49] The Alabama courts had laid down fairly strict rules of proof in 1891 (in *Ex parte Riley*, involving a white man who had bound out his son), and the legislature, after a few confirmatory cases, had responded with a "presumptive evidence" emendation.[50]

The Alabama statute was the one finally tested in the Supreme Court. The facts in the case are fairly well known; a bare outline is presented here.[51] Alonzo Bailey, a black man, entered a contract to perform services as a farm laborer for $12 a month. He received a $15 advance (to be deducted in monthly installments), but quit his job after working for one month and part of the next. Bailey was then indicted under the contract law, tried, convicted, and sentenced to 136 days at hard labor. (He was fined $30—this accounted for 20 days; the additional 116 days were added to his sentence for court costs and lawyers' fees.) With the help of interested Alabama Progressives, including a Montgomery city court justice, William H. Thomas, the case was appealed, first to the Alabama Supreme Court and subsequently, after some setbacks, to the United States Supreme Court.[52]

When that Court handed down its decision in 1911, Justice Hughes spoke for a seven-man majority. He "at once dismiss[ed] from consideration the fact that the plaintiff in error is a black man . . . [since] the statute on its face makes no racial discrimination. No question of a sectional character is presented, and we may view the legislation in the same manner as if it had been enacted in New York or in Idaho.[53] This outlook may seem absurd on its face, given the history of such statutes, but the Court was in no mood to listen to allegations of the discriminatory ap-

plication or effects of outwardly nondiscriminatory laws. Sociological jurisprudence had made its first inroads with the "Brandeis Brief," but such factual evidence was not accepted in cases
involving the civil rights of Negroes for another generation.
Thus, the "equal protection of the laws" argument was not considered.

Hughes then went on to consider the "presumptive evidence"
clause of the statute. He noted that the rule laid down in *Ex parte
Riley* had shown that as the intent of the accused can rarely be
made clear by direct evidence, the jury must ascertain intent
through inferences from the facts and circumstances developed
by the proof. In the absence of such inferences, the jury is not
"justified in indulging in mere unsupported conjectures, specu-
lations or suspicions as to intentions." However, the Alabama
Supreme Court had declared, "It is no doubt true that the
difficulty in proving the intent no doubt suggested the amendment . . . to the statute." Hughes noted that "the asserted
difficulty of proving the intent to injure or defraud is thus made
the occasion for dispensing with such proof." Further, the courts
of Alabama enforced a rule of evidence which denied the accused the right to testify "as to his uncommunicated motives,
purpose, or intention" in such cases.[54]

The sum of all this, in Hughes's eyes, was to make "the case
the same in effect as if the statute had made it a criminal act to
leave the service. . . . To say that he has been found guilty of an
intent to injure or defraud his employer, and not merely for
breaking his contract . . . is a distinction without a difference to
Bailey." He dismissed the argument of the Alabama court that
the jury was not controlled by the presumption—that is, that
they could find the accused innocent even without rebuttal of
the presumption. For Hughes, the fact that the "statute *au-
thorizes* the jury to convict" in such circumstances was enough to
convert it into a violation of the Thirteenth Amendment's prohibition against involuntary servitude.

> We cannot escape the conclusion that, although the statute in its
> term is to punish fraud, still its natural and inevitable effect is to
> expose to conviction for crime those who simply fail or refuse to
> perform contracts for personal service in liquidation of a debt;

and judging its purpose by its effect, that it seeks in this way to provide the means of compulsion through which performance of such service may be secured. . . . The words involuntary servitude have a "larger meaning than slavery." . . . What the state may not do directly it may not do indirectly. If it cannot punish the servant as a criminal for the mere failure or refusal to serve . . . it is not permitted to accomplish the same result by creating a statutory presumption which, upon proof of no other fact, exposes him to conviction and punishment.[55]

Surprisingly the "Great Dissenter," Justice Oliver Wendell Holmes, chose to exercise his predilection in this case. Holmes simply argued that the statute was no more than a punishment for fraud. It did not produce peonage, which required "bodily compulsion" by the master. The Thirteenth Amendment did not abolish labor contracts, and if an employer might use the threat of a civil suit for damages to induce the workman to perform service, why could not the state aid in that inducement by the imposition of a fine? Both have the same purpose—why prefer one to the other? Adding criminal liability to civil liability:

simply intensifies the legal motive for doing right; it does not make the laborer a slave. . . . I do not blink the fact that the liability to imprisonment may work as a motive . . . that . . . may induce the laborer to keep on when he would like to leave. . . . But it does not strike me as an objection to a law that it is effective. If the contract is one that ought not to be made, prohibit it. But if it is a perfectly fair and proper contract, I can see no reason why the state should not throw its weight on the side of performance.[56]

Hughes had argued that the fact that Bailey had worked for more than a month showed good faith; Holmes ignored this argument and stated that "if a man should receive an advance on a contract overnight, and leaves the next morning, is that not presumptive evidence of fraud?" (Both sides ignored the fact that no evidence had been introduced to show that Bailey had ever been paid his wages; that is, the odds were that he had just about paid off his debt.) It is true, said Holmes, that the statute was in more general terms than that, but this was only significant if we assumed "that this law is not administered as it would be in

New York, and that juries will act with prejudice against the laboring man. For prima facie evidence is only evidence, and as such may be held by the jury insufficient to make out guilt."[57] Thus, the statute, even with the Alabama rule of evidence, was constitutional.

It is difficult to see how this opinion fits into the general picture we have of Justice Holmes. He seems contemptuous of the majority's claim that they had ignored racial and sectional factors in making their decision. Had he demanded evidence that the law was administered unfairly, it might have been understandable. However, we know that Holmes was bored silly by his first contact with the "Brandeis Brief"; he had also said, "I hate facts."[58] That being so, this opinion seems to be a legalistic exercise for its own sake. Holmes, it is true, did have great respect for the powers of the states, but (as his later opinions show) not to the point of overlooking gross abuses of those powers in regard to individual rights. He is undoubtedly correct when he notes that a similar decision would not have been likely if the law in question had been on the books in New York; the majority was really fudging the issue, to avoid the Fourteenth Amendment question among other reasons. One is still struck, however, by the empty rhetoric of Holmes's ritualism in this case.

In 1914 the Supreme Court dealt with its last peonage case of this period, *U.S.* v. *Reynolds.* This case revolved around the southern practice of "confessing judgment"—the criminal surety system. These are newer phrases for our old friend, the private convict-labor contract, which enabled a convicted criminal to work out his fine in the employ of one who paid his fine. Alabama, out in the open with its laws, had gone one step further than the other states that countenanced this practice and had enacted a surety statute. This law made "failure to perform a contract with surety . . . [after] confessing judgment for fine and costs," a crime, punishable by a fine of "not less than the amount of damages which the party contracting with him has suffered by such failure or refusal."[59] Of course, this new amount was, in practice, simply added to the old, and the laborer could then make a new contract with either his old employer or a different claimant for his services.

It was argued, even by Progressives like Ray Stannard Baker, that the surety system enabled the black to avoid jail through the kindly intervention of some (white) patron.[60] Baker goes so far as to argue that the worst aspect of the system was that it encouraged blacks to think that the laws did not really apply to them, as they never went to jail for petty crime. In actual operation these laws served to place the "confessed' felon into a state of permanent bondage.

The legal defense of the statute lay in a simple premise—namely that the surety had become the agent of the state in extracting from the convict the fine he owed to the state. The labor thus performed, even though coerced, was punishment for crime, not forced labor for debt. Because "involuntary servitude" as a punishment for crime was specifically excluded from the prohibitions of the Thirteenth Amendment, the system was constitutional.

On the other hand, the state had no interest in the contract; in fact the Alabama Supreme Court said, "The state is in no sense a party to the contract, it permitted the making of the contract and provides a punishment for its breach."[61] Further, the state does not proceed against the prisoner for its fine, but rather for the damages suffered by the employer. The nature of the labor performed was not prescribed by the statute, nor was it supervised either by or for the benefit of the state.

The Supreme Court brushed aside the arguments of the defense. The statute was, in the court's mind, nothing more than a means of ensuring performance of a contract of service. The relation of debtor to creditor was created, and punishment was provided for breach of a contract based on that relation. "Compulsion of such service by the constant fear of imprisonment under the criminal laws renders the work compulsory."[62]

Furthermore, had the convict chosen to work out his fine in the county workhouse, he would have earned seventy-five cents per day; in the instant case, he had contracted to work for six dollars *a month*. Since the new fine for breach could be worked out under a new surety contract, a breach of this latest contract would again be prosecuted in a similar manner. Thus, "under pain of recurring prosecution, the convict may be kept at labor to satisfy the demands of his employer. The convict is thus kept chained to an ever-turning wheel of servitude to discharge the obligation which he has incurred."[63]

Justice Holmes, concurring separately, was malleable but unrepentant. He reiterated that there was no reason a state could not call such actions fraud, but agreed that people are "impulsive" and will "relieve present pain" by engaging to suffer future agonies. Simply to prevent this, he rather condescendingly agreed to the decision, if not the reasoning, of the Court.[64]

Alabama had gone further than other states in promulgating this particular law. Although the supportive law itself was unique, the system was widespread and it seemed to work well without the aid of a surety law. The private convict-labor contract, as noted earlier, had been around for quite some time. What might have happened to the system had extensive challenges been made to its standard operation is an interesting, if unanswerable question. For with this case, the Court got out of the peonage business for almost thirty years. The first thrust against peonage by the federal government was over.

# 6
# After *Bailey*

*Thus it appears that Cook was arrested . . . solely on account of his failure to comply with his contract. . . . Even if this is true . . . defendants cannot be convicted . . . of peonage.*

Taylor v. U.S. *(1917)*

The decision in *Bailey* v. *Alabama* had been hailed as a marked step forward in the battle against peonage. By Ray Stannard Baker it was seen as a second Dred Scott case, a start for a great push against an obnoxious practice. It was confidently expected that similar statutes on the books of other states would now be declared invalid and that sinister operation of the peonage system would soon cease.[1]

However, several factors militated against this happy result. First among these was the fact that only one sort of peonage law had been declared unconstitutional—the sort containing the presumptive evidence clause. A state that dropped this clause, or did not have it, could still prosecute debtors for accepting advances fraudulently. (As an additional fillip, since the Alabama rule of evidence regarding the defendant's testimony had played a significant part in the *Bailey* decision, the state courts could still distinguish their statutes from the Alabama law on that basis.)

Further, the only sort of peonage which had been attacked was that which involved debt, "the basal fact of peonage" in the narrow definition given to it by the Supreme Court. There were other sorts of forced labor, closely akin to this, which were not covered by this definition. Assistant Attorney General Russell had anticipated this problem as far back as 1907 and had suggested passage of a new law forbidding "involuntary servitude and all attempts at it," abandoning use of the word *peonage* altogether.[2] This advice had not been taken by the Congress. No attack had been made on the labor-enticement laws either, and these remained untouched by the flurry of federal anti-peonage activities.

Perhaps more important, the push behind the federal government's interest in the area was dissipated. With the election of Woodrow Wilson as president, the emphasis placed on peonage by Roosevelt and Taft was shifted to other areas. Complaints of peonage were still received, but few prosecutions were brought. It is doubtful that Georgia, for instance, would have been able to "finesse" the *Bailey* decision without the indifference of the federal government. Perhaps the neglect was "benign" in nature, from the government's point of view; a noncontemporary can never know. Certainly, the effect was not—from the viewpoint of the helpless black laborer.

None of this should be taken to indicate that the decisions of the Supreme Court had had no effect. Alabama's laws had, of course, been struck down. Within months the legislature had placed a new law on the books, but without a "presumptive evidence" section. South Carolina, in an apparent response to *Bailey*, dropped its presumption clause. In Mississippi and North Carolina the state courts declared their respective laws unconstitutional.[3] It should be clear that none of these actions really reduced peonage; they simply made it more difficult to prove fraudulent intent in the few situations where both trial and appeal took place. The threat of trial was usually sufficient, and there was almost absolute certainty of conviction at the trial court level. If the rules of proof set down by the state supreme courts had been applied, of course, most of these cases would have been dismissed. But the likelihood of appeal (and reversal) was so slight, given the circumstances of the accused, that no one seemed to worry about it. However, these states did, at least formally, comply with the rulings of the Supreme Court.

Georgia and Florida, on the other hand, were almost openly defiant. Georgia's contract law was essentially on a par with that of Alabama.[4] It contained a similar presumptive evidence clause and was otherwise on all fours with it. The Georgia courts had, of course, vehemently defended this law in the past.[5] Now, the question was, how would they react to the *Bailey* decision?

In the first case to deal with the question, *Latson* v. *Wells*, the Georgia Supreme Court was able to escape without a hand being laid on it. The *Bailey* decision was raised by the plaintiff in error, but the courts had a defense tactic available. First, the court described the act as one intended only to punish fraud, and, therefore, clearly free of the taint put on the Alabama statute by the Supreme Court. Further, the *Bailey* case had hinged upon the presumptive evidence clause. Georgia, it was conceded, did have a similar clause, but its constitutionality was not relevant, as Latson had pleaded guilty to the charges, intending to test the law itself. Since the facts had never gone to the jury, the constitutionality of the second clause was not in question. The two sections were clearly separable, said the court; one set out the nature of the offense; the second, the rules of proof to be used in a trial. Latson could not "properly contend that he pleaded guilty because if he had gone to trial, an unconstitutional act relating to a rule of evidence would have been used against him," for, if the rule were unconstitutional, "it is presumed the court trying him would have so declared."[6] Heaving a sigh of relief, the justices confirmed the conviction.

In *Wilson* v. *State*, however, no such easy way out was presented. The accused had been tried, using the presumption section of the act. Furthermore, like Alabama, Georgia also had a rule about the testimony of the defendant in such cases. It did not prevent him from testifying about his motives, as in *Bailey;* it prevented him from testifying *altogether*.[7] If the Georgia law was to be sustained this time, the court would have to work to sustain it. Yet it had, it seems, little difficulty in meeting the challenge.

As a start, the court reiterated its earlier interpretation of the meaning of the first section: that it was intended only to punish fraud and was clearly constitutional. As an additional precedent, of course, it now used the *Latson* case. Again, using *Latson*, the entire second section was declared a mere "rule of evidence" and thereby wholly severable from the first.[8] Therefore, even should this latter section, at some time in the future, be declared invalid, it would have no effect on the former, which could "stand independently of the latter." Having covered the bases in case of a future United States court reversal, the Georgia court now proceeded to uphold the second section. Ignoring Hughes's strictures in *Bailey*, the court argued that there was no reason why the state could not prescribe the elements of proof to be used in a trial. The court cited a sentence from Hughes's opinion, but pointedly ignored the fact that he had demolished that argument in the next three paragraphs. What had been a "straw man" for Hughes, became gospel in *Wilson* v. *State*. The discussion in *Bailey* of the Alabama rule of evidence, although not basic to the decision, now bore bitter fruit. The presumption clause was therefore ruled valid, unless there was a similar rule of evidence attached to it.

Since Georgia did have a similar rule, the problem of distinguishing *Bailey* now arose. (It had been mentioned only briefly in the major portion of the opinion.) The court proceeded to do so. "In the first place, the Alabama statute provided that 'Any person who with intent to injure or defraud his employer,' etc." The Georgia statute punished only those who intended to defraud; "We do not stop to discuss whether the mere attempt to injure may be different from the intent to defraud," the court declared, but it did stop to make it a distinguishable point.[9] Secondly, the Alabama statute gave half the fine to the employer; the Georgia statute did not. A truthful if wholly insignificant point, it was not discussed in *Bailey*. Finally, the court declared that the essence of the *Bailey* decision rested on the Alabama rule that barred testimony on intent by the accused. The Georgia rule did not permit the accused to testify at all, but he was permitted to use the old common law right to make a statement, not under oath, to the court.[10] This statement was to have "such force as the jury may think right to give it and 'they may believe it in preference to the sworn testimony in the case.'" If this last line (a quotation from *Bailey*) sounds familiar, it should be remembered that Hughes had found himself "not impressed with the argument that . . . the jury is not controlled by the presumption, if unrebutted, and still may find the accused not guilty."[11] The Georgia court, however, apparently *was* impressed by its own reasoning and declared the statute distinguishable and valid.[12]

It seems doubtful that anyone expected this juridical pap to stand up in the Supreme Court. The case notes call the approach "interesting," but question whether it could stand, considering the nature of Justice Hughes's opinion in *Bailey*.[13] The time and effort put in by the Georgia court to declare the two portions of the statute severable indicate that even the justices themselves held out no great hope for their ruling. The ruling remained in force for thirty years. *Wilson* was never appealed to the federal courts, and the Georgia statute was safe.

In Florida, on the other hand, the legislature simply defied both the federal and the state courts—and won out by sheer persistence. It is true that, after the early Florida peonage cases, the legislature had dropped its contract-labor laws from the books. However, in 1913 a new statute was passed. It tried to take the *Bailey* decision into account, at least as far as the presumption clause went, but it did so abominably. In the first place, its composition was so careless that it seemed to have been written on the back of an old envelope or some other piece of scrap paper, for it contained such phrases as "fail or refuse to pay for the money . . . received."[14] Secondly, it tried to make the failure to fulfill a labor contract presumptive evidence of guilt without saying it in so many words. This statute came before the Florida Supreme Court four years after passage in *Goode* v. *Nelson*, and that body had no difficulty in wiping it off the books. The court, citing *Bailey* and *Clyatt*, declared that the act did not punish fraud, but rather refusal to perform service. It was, therefore, on all fours with the Alabama statute invalidated in *Bailey* and violative of "the organic law"—that is, the United States Constitution.[15] The court distinguished attacks on real fraud, such as cases of embezzlement, from criminal punishment for simple breach of contract—in brief, a model opinion in the circumstances.

The legislature was not to be denied, however, and passed another law in 1919. This time it dropped all pretense and virtually copied the Alabama statute. Section 1, however, did not include any reference to a *refusal* to perform service, it simply described a fraudulent receipt of advances, "under and by reason of a contract or promise to perform labor."[16] Section 2 contained the usual prima facie evidence section, resurrected from the act dropped after the *Clyatt* decision, and on a par with the statute revoked in *Bailey*.

When this act was challenged in 1922, it seemed to stand little chance of survival since four of the five justices of the Florida Supreme Court then sitting had participated in the earlier case of *Goode* v. *Nelson* in 1917.[17] Any such conjectures proved to be premature, however, for in *Phillips* v. *Bell*, the court upheld the statute. First the justices indulged themselves in citing some supposedly significant distinctions between the Florida and Alabama statutes. After this ritual they declared that the two sections of the act were clearly separable. They did not even attempt to defend the latter section (in fact they gave every indication that it was unconstitutional), but declined to rule upon it. "As none of the testimony introduced in County Judge's Court is brought here . . . there is nothing on record to show that in the trial, the rule of evidence [the prima facie clause] laid down in Section 2 was applied."[18] Thus, since there was nothing to show that "satisfactory proof of a fraudulent scheme was not adduced," the court could duck the issue of the validity of the second section.[19] The conviction of Phillips was upheld and the statute stood until 1944.

Both *Phillips* and *Goode* were unanimous decisions—how the same personnel could reach such diverse conclusions on the validity of reasonably similar statutes is something of a mystery. Was it simply the persistence of the legislature? The rapidly building evidence of federal indifference? Had political pressures on the justices built up over the years? Whatever the reasons, the reversal was complete, and Florida joined Georgia in defying the Supreme Court in words as well as substance. The maneuvers of the Florida legislature in regard to the qualifications of judges sitting on contract-labor cases should be recalled.

This sort of judicial activity was the exception, not the rule. In most of the South, the appellate courts either reluctantly followed the lead of the Supreme Court and declared peonage laws unconstitutional, or so modified the laws under challenge as to bring them into line with the Constitution through judicial amendment. In Louisiana the courts tried to put off meeting the challenge for some time, and in this they were aided by a peculiarity of state law. The appellate jurisdiction of the Louisiana Supreme Court was limited to two classes of criminal cases, one "whenever the punishment of death or imprisonment at hard labor *may be* inflicted," and the other whenever "a fine exceeding three hundred dollars, or imprisonment exceeding six months, is actually imposed."[20] Thus, unless the trial judge exceeded those limits of punishment in his sentence, declared the law unconstitutional, or quashed the indictment himself, the Louisiana Supreme Court could avoid such issues. As no trial judge had done any of these things up to 1918, the contract-labor statute still was untouched at that time.[21] However, during that year two justices, Judge W. W. Bailey of the Seventeenth Judicial District and Judge W. S. Rownd of the Twenty-fifth, quashed indictments brought under the contract-labor statute.[22] For some reason, perhaps the double-barreled nature of the attack, the state appealed, and the Louisiana Supreme Court had to face the issue. Once forced to this extreme, the court saw no alternative to declaring the statute unconstitutional. Citing *Bailey*, an admirably brief opinion reversed the earlier controlling case, *State* v. *Murray*, and invalidated the act.[23]

In brief, except in Georgia, Florida, and parts of North Carolina, the contract-labor laws had to operate on the basis of fraudulent intent and without the presumptive evidence clause.[24] On the other hand, the enticement statutes had never undergone a serious challenge. They were brought to the appellate courts in the post-*Bailey* period, but their constitutionality was always upheld.[25] Ten states of the South had enticement statutes on their books in this period, and they were unique to the region.[26]

Although the state courts upheld the constitutionality of the enticement laws, they followed the now familiar pattern of treating those cases that reached the appellate level with great caution. In two states the statutes were essentially amended by judicial construction. In South Carolina the question was raised in *Shaw* v. *Fisher*.[27] An employee of the plaintiff, a cropper named Carver, had left the plantation after five months of labor and had subsequently been hired by the defendant (and others in the community). Carver had signed a contract to work for a year, and the defendant had been successfully sued for damages in the lower court for committing the common law tort of employing or harboring a runaway servant.[28] The case revolved around the question of whether a subsequent employer (or harborer) of such a servant was liable even if the termination of service had been a voluntary and independent act on the part of the laborer. Both statute law and a long line of precedents supported such claims of liability. However, the South Carolina Supreme Court, after a review of *Bailey* and *Clyatt*, declared that the Thirteenth and Fourteenth amendments had "superseded" and annulled all statutory or common law in conflict with them. Thus the common law had been modified to bar actions in cases where no enticement had taken place. As long as the termination of service by the laborer was voluntary, the second employer was free to hire him without threat of legal redress by the original employer.[29]

In Mississippi the statutory law underwent similar judicial emendation. The controlling case had been *Armistead* v. *Chatters*, in which the enticement statute had been upheld and its punitive provisions liberally applied against the subsequent employer.[30] In *Beale* v. *Yazoo Yarn Mill*, however, the Mississippi Supreme Court required that proof of actual enticement must be shown in order to convict, and thus, in 1921, distinguished *Armistead*. Five years later the court added a demand that knowledge of the laborer's previous contract must be proved. Finally, in *Thompson* v. *Box*, the *Armistead* case was overruled.[31] Citing *Bailey*, the court held that unless a strict and "reasonable" construction were placed on the statute, it might be in conflict with the United States Constitution. If the *Armistead* precedent were followed, "the darkies in the case at bar," having abandoned their service, would find "the hand of every man" against them, and would be forced to "stay or starve." This might be seen as a form of slavery, and the statute could then be put in jeopardy. It was, in the court's mind, "our duty to uphold a statute, if possible, by placing a reasonable construction thereon which would render said statute harmonious with both the federal and state constitutions. . . . The construction we have placed upon the statute leaves it on our books, freed from constitutional objection."[32]

It was, of course, equally true (if unstated) that such construction essentially permitted the law to operate in the real world just as it had done in the past. The statute remained on the books; it read just as it had before. The likelihood that local justices of the peace or laborers (or employers for that matter) would be aware of such judicial legislation was slim indeed. Thus the court had successfully manipulated the enticement statute into a safe refuge from constitutional attack, while enabling the coercion to continue as usual except where decisions were appealed. Further, the laws themselves were only statements of the unwritten rules of the game, which gave a social stigma to those who hired the laborers of another; the code of the planter forbade it.[33] These judicial emendations of the law provided relief only for those select few who could reach the higher courts; they did little for the average farm laborer.

Despite the general indifference to peonage, there were several exposés of the practice which drew widespread publicity. The most spectacular of these was the infamous "murder farm" trial in Jasper County, Georgia. Two federal agents had been investigating charges of peonage at the plantation of John Williams, a Georgia planter.[34] Williams specialized in using the criminal surety system to provide himself with cheap labor. After the agents left his farm, Williams (quite understandably, since he ran a brutal slave farm) feared possible federal prosecution for peonage. He therefore silenced the potential witnesses against him (his peons) by the simplest of means—he had them murdered. (Farmer Williams was unduly alarmed, for the federal agents had been convinced by his "frankness" and reported the charges unfounded.) The subsequent trial (by the state) on murder charges, produced sensational headlines and revelations. After Williams was convicted of murder, Hugh M. Dorsey, a former governor of Georgia, published a pamphlet delineating southern lawlessness towards the black laborer. It was a stunning exposé of peonage, lynchings, and so forth.[35] Although the trial itself had brought forth much popular outcry against an isolated instance of brutality and peonage, this sort of general attack on the practice produced a wholly different reaction. Dorsey was vilified as a slanderer and a villain who "defiles his mother— Georgia."[36] The pamphlet, and the exposé, soon disappeared into limbo.

The last major incident of the twenties bringing peonage to public attention was the Mississippi flood of 1927. The rising waters forced hundreds of thousands of refugees to take shelter in emergency camps all along the river delta. The relief efforts were coordinated by the then secretary of commerce, Herbert Hoover, with the assistance of the American Red Cross and similar agencies.[37] Before the flood waters had subsided, the camps had become peonage centers for the blacks. Compelled to live in unbelievable conditions, they became a source of forced labor for anyone who wanted them. They, and they alone, had to work on the levees, but more significantly, the National Guard also forced them to work for plantation owners and others. The "relief" camps became employment agencies for the agricultural entrepreneur. Although the conditions were investigated (by a Colored Advisory Commission), the report was suppressed. The state and federal agencies involved worked hand in hand to maintain "the system," and only the rather impotent and pathetic outrage of the NAACP caused the slightest upset.

In the thirties, there appeared a variety of exposés of black sharecropping and tenantry, but most of these were more sociological than legal in nature.[38] They did expose the conditions of southern agriculture, however, and made clear the need for legal action, particularly on the part of the federal government.

Such prodding was clearly necessary, for in the Department of Justice, once a hotbed of antipeonage activity, the attitude towards peon masters seemed to be live and let live. The Georgia "murder farm" incident was typical; government agents had investigated the complaint and reported it unjustified. The fact that the very threat of the investigation had caused the plantation owner to murder eleven potential witnesses against him was embarrassing, but it seemed to cause no great change in the department's operations. This general laxity seems to go back to the Wilson era, when southern influence had become more noticeable. It is in this period that the short-lived federal interest in peonage was blunted and de-emphasized. Clearly, Wilson's administration had little desire to embarrass its southern allies. The special peonage section of the Justice Department was allowed to lie fallow and eventually disappear. Further, the severest judicial blow to the government's attack on peonage also occurred in this period, in *Taylor* v. *United States*, with the apparent acquiescence of the administration.[39]

The facts of the case were simple. They involved a "young, white man" named Willie Cook. (This is one of the rare instances in which all parties in the case were white, which perhaps explains why the case was appealed.) Cook went to a farmer named J. G. Taylor and borrowed thirteen dollars from him in order to get married. At the same time, he signed a contract to labor for

Taylor for a period of one year at the rate of ten dollars per month. (Even in those days, this was an incredibly low wage.) Cook worked for two months and then, finding himself unable to live on his salary, went to see his father-in-law. The two men went to Taylor in order to try to free the young husband from the contract. Taylor at first declined, but then agreed to release him if he would pay back the loan and an additional twenty-five dollars for "damages." Before any payment was made, however, Taylor went to a local magistrate, one Ioor Hayes, and got him to write a letter to Cook which threatened prosecution if he failed to return to work. Hayes told the two men, when they came to see him, that he could do nothing for them; they must "fix it up with Taylor." After some discussion, an agreement was reached. Cook pleaded guilty to violation of section 492 of the South Carolina Criminal Code: "Any person who shall contract with another to render . . . personal service of any kind, and shall thereafter fraudulently, or with malicious intent to injure his employer, fail or refuse to render such service as agreed upon, shall be deemed guilty of a misdemeanor." [40]

Hayes accepted twenty-five dollars in payment from Cook's father-in-law and the matter seemed closed. However, five days later, Hayes issued a warrant for Cook's arrest and announced to the distraught defendant that he must either work for Taylor or serve "on the chain gang for the rest of the year." (This double-cross was probably a result of the fact that Hayes did not turn over the money to Taylor but considered it a fine.) Cook refused and was sentenced to thirty days at hard labor. At the end of this period, Hayes announced that, although the contract was for a year, the wages were paid monthly, and he considered the contract a monthly one. Therefore he would issue a fresh warrant every month, with a similar sentence, unless Cook returned to Taylor's farm. At this point, the federal government intervened and tried both Taylor and Hayes for violation of the Anti-Peonage Act ("returning . . . to a condition of peonage") and conspiracy to do so. [41] They were convicted, but appealed to the Circuit Court, which promptly overturned the convictions.

The court found that there was no element of debt in the case, and debt was "the basal fact" of peonage. [42] It was conceded that part of Taylor's original claim was based on the debt of thirteen dollars, but the court found that this debt had been extinguished by the payment of twenty-five dollars to Magistrate Hayes. Although Hayes himself had treated this sum as a fine and eventually turned it over to the county treasurer, the justices found that Hayes, in that instance, had merely acted "as the agent of Taylor" in accepting the sum. Thus, the subsequent conviction and sentencing of Cook had been purely on the basis of his failure to fulfill his contract. (The fact that this had been either an unconstitutional application of the law, or the application of an unconstitutional law, was not considered germane to the case.) "An obligation to work, we think, cannot be reasonably construed to mean a debt as contemplated by the peonage statute."

Even if Hayes had entered into some agreement with Taylor to force Cook to work for him, he was not liable to prosecution, "inasmuch as it clearly appears that . . . Cook had paid every cent of the money that he owed Taylor."[43] The defendants might be guilty of something, the court was not sure what, but they were not guilty of peonage.

This was a split decision, the court dividing two to one (Justice Woods dissented). The reasoning of the majority seemed a bit shaky and open to challenge. However, the efforts of United States Attorney Francis H. Weston, who had argued the case before the Circuit Court, to appeal, were unavailing. President Wilson's solicitor general, John W. Davis, scotched this plan, saying that a "technicality," whose nature he did not state, prevented appeal.[44] The extremely narrow definition of peonage given in *Taylor* was thus ensconced as a valid precedent—not so significant in terms of law as it proved to be in offering an excuse for federal agents to dismiss complaints as unfounded.

Justice (both in the sense of the Department and of the concept) was no longer much concerned with the practice of peonage. To be sure, there are a scattering of federal indictments and convictions in the thirty years after *Bailey*, but they are the rare exceptions to the rule of indifference. However, as the thirties drew to a close, new pressures caused both a revival of federal interest and a resurrection of some Civil War statutes, resulting in a second thrust against peonage.

# 7
# The Civil Rights Section

*If such statutes have ever on even one occasion been put to a worthier use in the records of any state court, it has not been called to our attention.*

Pollock *v.* Williams *(1944)*

Shortly after his appointment as attorney general of the United States in 1939, Frank Murphy announced the establishment of a special unit in the Criminal Division of the Department of Justice. The Civil Liberties Unit was given the responsibility to "direct, supervise and conduct prosecutions of violations of the provisions of the Constitution or Acts of Congress guaranteeing civil rights to individuals."[1] The creation of this unit was the result of a period of internecine warfare within the department —a tale too complicated for inclusion here. The new unit was placed under the direction of Henry A. Schweinhaut, who had been a leading light in the unsuccessful (but significant) prosecutions in the Harlan County Labor Trial. The unit's title was soon changed to the Civil Rights Section (CRS).

One of the first tasks assigned to the CRS was to examine and study the legal problems arising from civil rights statutes, and one of the first issues listed for review was peonage.[2] The section was determined to attack the problems of forced labor, but in order to do so it had to clarify the legal tools with which it could work.[3] Just how difficult a task this would be was presaged by the fact that even the initial memorandum describing what was to be done gave an incorrect definition of peonage.[4]

Assistant Attorney General Brian McMahon, the author of the memorandum, managed to uncover three successful prosecutions in the period 1936–1939 to list under the heading of peonage. However, one of the three was the case of *U.S.* v.

*Peacher* (E.D. Ark. 1937, unreported) in which a conviction was gained on a charge of slavery. The difference in definition was one of the problems that had to be dealt with. It was, perhaps, even more discouraging to note that the fourth (and last) item under this heading was a report of a federal investigation into peonage in Alabama. The assistant to the attorney general found conditions "to be very bad," succeeded in convincing the governor to pardon a number of wrongfully convicted peons—and concluded by saying that his personal investigations had proved the complaints to be groundless!

The first problem lay in the wording of the traditional tool—the Anti-Peonage Act. As written, it punished anyone who "holds, arrests, returns . . . any person *to* a condition of peonage."[5] No one was quite sure how the preposition "to" was supposed to fit in the sentence; it seemed to be intended to follow all three verbs. What did holding or arresting "to" peonage mean? One conviction had already been overturned by the phrasing of "returning to" peonage (*Clyatt* v. *United States*) and it was necessary to determine whether or not the other two phrases applied where the individual had not previously been placed in a condition of peonage.[6]

The most vexing problem of all with regard to this statute was the fact that a peonage charge must contain an element of debt—the "basal fact" of peonage. As far back as 1907, Assistant Attorney General Russell had argued that the Supreme Court, in the *Clyatt* case, had misconstrued the act by borrowing its definition from an 1857 case in New Mexico. As a realist, however, he had also suggested that a new law barring involuntary servitude, regardless of debt, be passed. As this had aroused no response, Russell then anticipated his successors and tried a peon master for slavery.[7]

It was this idea that struck the CRS researchers as an alternative means of conviction where no debt could be shown. In 1936 Paul D. Peacher, an Arkansas sheriff, had been convicted of violation of the 1866 Slave-Kidnapping Act. The Southern Tenant Farmers' Union had applied enough pressure to help force an indictment, and the government had taken the unusual step of trying the case under this act.[8] This success seemed to give the section a new tool, but it was shrouded in obscurity. The act punished anyone who "kidnaps or carries away" any person, with the intent that he "be sold into involuntary servitude, or held as a slave."[9] The problem lay in the definition of the word *slave*. If the Court interpreted the language broadly, almost any person held in detention (except upon lawful conviction for a criminal act) would be covered. If, however, the term was restricted to individuals held as personal property, the act would be virtually useless. At this time, the only judicial definition of *slave* had been given in the strikingly unsuccessful case of *U.S.* v. *Sabbia*. The question was thus left open, but the CRS determined to use the statute.

In addition, the CRS could call upon sections of Title 18, which punished conspiracy to deprive citizens of their civil rights (Section 51), and participation of public officials in such deprivations (Section 52). Finally, Section 88 of Title 18, a general conspiracy statute, might be employed. In 1941 Attorney General Francis Biddle issued instructions to all United States attorneys that the Slave-Kidnapping Act and Sections 51, 52, and 88 should be used in preference to the Anti-Peonage Act. This was indicated by "a survey of Department files on alleged peonage violations" which disclosed wholesale instances where prosecution was declined by the United States attorney.[10] If debt was so difficult to prove, Biddle reasoned, forget it and use involuntary servitude in its stead.

While this maneuvering was going on, peonage was getting increased publicity. In addition to the NAACP and the Southern Tenant Farmers' Union (old friends to the cause), the International Labor Defense (ILD) now formed the Abolish Peonage Committee of America. (The ILD had been organized by the Communist party in 1925.) The Abolish Peonage Committee was applying pressure for the prosecution of a peon master named Cunningham. The Justice Department at first refused to prosecute the case, Attorney General Jackson declaring that there was no violation of the peonage statute. In the end Cunningham was indicted under the general conspiracy statute, but the charge was vacated by a federal judge in Georgia.[11]

In 1941 all this activity finally bore fruit. The Georgia labor-contract statute had been challenged, and the Georgia courts had continued to maintain its validity. In *Taylor* v. *State* the

Georgia Supreme Court rather contemptuously dismissed the appeal.[12] It simply cited the line of state cases which preceded the *Bailey* decision and then concluded with a special mention of *Wilson* v. *State*. (This last, it will be recalled, was the 1912 case in which the court had denied the applicability of *Bailey* to the Georgia law.) In this case, however, an appeal was taken to the United States Supreme Court, and the modern observer finds himself struck with a distinct sense of déjà vu. Fully thirty years after the *Bailey* decision was handed down, the case is essentially reargued. The same tired claims that the statute does nothing more than punish fraud, that the presumptive evidence clause is merely a rule of evidence, and so on, are made again by the state. Fortunately, if only for the sake of sanity, the decision of the Court was equally reminiscent.

Justice James F. Byrnes, a southerner himself, wrote the opinion for a unanimous Court in *Taylor* v. *Georgia*. If the Georgia court had dismissed the appeal with a casual listing of largely pre-*Bailey* precedents, the Supreme Court was just as casual in dismissing Georgia's arguments.

> It is argued here, just as it was in the Bailey case, that the purpose of #7408 is nothing more than the punishment of a species of fraud.... And the presumption created by #7409 is said to be merely a rule of evidence for the trial of cases arising under #7408. Actually, however, #7409 embodies a substantive prohibition which squarely contravenes the Thirteenth Amendment and the Act of Congress of March 2, 1867 ... [the Anti-Peonage Act]. There is no material distinction between the Georgia statutes challenged here and the Alabama statute which was held to violate the Thirteenth Amendment in *Bailey* v. *Alabama*.[13]

Byrnes dismissed the *Wilson* precedent with dispatch: the Georgia court had given it validity because of "a misconception of the scope of the *Bailey* decision."[14] The parallels between the Georgia and Alabama laws seem as obvious to the casual reader as they did to the Supreme Court; one is led to wonder why the statute had been permitted to rest unchallenged for thirty years. In any case, the period of neglect at this level was now over.

However, the capacity of the federal courts to overturn state laws that enforced peonage had never been in question; what had happened to the somewhat limited and insecure legal arsenal the CRS had created for positive action? In *United States* v. *Gaskin*, the "sword" aspect of the Anti-Peonage Act received further judicial construction. The question to be resolved was whether or not the mere seizure of an individual for the purpose of placing him in peonage was covered by the 1867 law. Gaskin had arrested a black man who, he claimed, owed him twenty dollars, and had transported him to his turpentine farm in northern Florida. The black, one Johnson, escaped before he had been forced to perform any labor. As a result of the escape (and the telling of the tale), Gaskin was indicted on a charge of arresting Johnson "to a condition of peonage." A United States District Court quashed the indictment on the grounds that the Anti-Peonage Act did not punish an arrest to compel service unless the person arrested actually does render such service. In an eight-to-one decision, the Supreme Court ruled that the act did cover such actions even where the intent is not achieved. The Court conceded that the language of the statute was "inartistic. The appropriate qualifying preposition for the word 'holds' is 'in.' An accurate qualifying phrase for the verb 'arrests' would be 'to place in or return to' peonage. But the compactness of phrasing and the lack of strict grammatical construction does not obscure the intent of the Act." The Court reviewed the history of the statute and the holding in *Clyatt*, and it concluded that the principle of strict construction of the law "does not require distortion or nullification of the evident purpose of the legislation." [15]

Both the argument and the history cited are compelling; it was all the more striking that the lone dissenter was Justice Frank Murphy, who had acquired a close following of liberals on the grounds that he was "a guy who votes right." As if to refute his dissent in the *Screws* case, where he bitterly objected to a reversal of a conviction on narrow technical grounds, Murphy, for some reason, decided to emulate Justice Frankfurter's stance in other cases and denied that the statute prohibited unsuccessful seizure for peonage. He called the majority opinion an "apologia for inadequate legislative draftsmanship" and, ignoring the decision in *Clyatt*, argued that no one could reasonably be expected to understand the statute to cover "an arrest not followed by actual peonage."[16] (Murphy's pleas for the application of common sense in the *Screws* case seem totally appropriate here. Whether or not his strictures were accurate, when the *United States Code* was revised in 1947 the wording of the statute *was* changed to follow the more "appropriate" phrasing suggested by the majority.)

Four months later the Supreme Court handed down a far more significant decision in *Pollock* v. *Williams*.[17] At the state court level, this case, like *Taylor* v. *Georgia*, was reminiscent of the cases of the immediate post-*Bailey* era. In *Williams* v. *Pollock*, the Florida Supreme Court had simply reiterated the arguments made in *Phillips* v. *Bell*, over twenty years before.[18] The state argued that the guilty plea precluded any consideration of the presumptive evidence clause, and that the two sections of the act were severable, in any case. No defense of the presumption section was offered at all.

The decision of the United States Supreme Court was handed down by Justice Robert Jackson, who, as attorney general, had aroused the wrath of the Anti-Peonage Committee for his lukewarm enforcement of the antipeonage laws. Now Jackson demonstrated what a difference a robe makes. First he reviewed the history of federal peonage legislation and introduced his famous analogy of "a shield and a sword." He then examined the history of peonage in Florida. Jackson noted the variety of violations of the federal statutes that had occurred in that state and the fact that at least four different contract-labor statutes had been enacted by the legislature over the years. Since "the present Act is the latest of a lineage," Jackson found it necessary to shift the burden of proof to the state.[19] Thus the state was required to demonstrate that the presumption section did not contribute to exacting the guilty plea. (The state had earlier, of course, simply argued that there was no evidence to the contrary.) The inference Jackson drew was simple: "The Florida legislature has enacted and twice re-enacted it [the prima facie evidence section] since we [decided *Bailey*]. We cannot assume it was doing an idle thing. Since the presumption was known to be unconstitutional and of no use in a contested case, the only explanation we can find for its persistent appearance in the statute is its extralegal coercive effect in suppressing defenses."

He then went on to describe how this section would affect a prosecution, especially in a court presided over by a layman, who was not likely to declare it unconstitutional.[20] At this point, however, Jackson began to enter virgin territory in the battle against peonage. *Bailey* had been widely assumed to have hinged on the presumptive evidence clause. Jackson now construed it, seemingly, to bar *all* contract-labor statutes:

> Where peonage has existed in the United States it has done so chiefly by virtue of laws like the statute in question. Whether the statute did or did not include the presumption seems to have made little difference in its practical effect. . . . It is a mistake to believe that in dealing with statutes of this type we have held the presumption section to be the only source of invalidity. On the contrary, the substantive section has contributed largely to the conclusion of unconstitutionality of the presumption section.[21]

Jackson also contemptuously dismissed the arguments that the statute was merely intended to punish common fraud. It was possible, he conceded, that a laborer might collect advances from several employers with no intent to perform service, or perhaps continue to hire himself out and collect advances in perpetuity:

> But in not one of the cases to come before this Court under the antipeonage statute has there been evidence of such subtlety of design. In each there was the same story, a necessitous and illiterate laborer, an agreement to work for a small wage, a trifling advance, a breach of contract to work. In not one has there been proof from which we fairly could say whether the Negro never intended to work out the advance, or quit because of some real or fancied grievance, or just got tired. If such statutes have ever on even one occasion been put to a worthier use in the records of any state court, it has not been called to our attention. If this is the visible record, it is hardly to be assumed that the off-the-record uses are more benign.[22]

It is doubtful that the emptiness of the argument made in defense of contract-labor laws could be more clearly demonstrated than it is in this one paragraph. Unfortunately, Jackson blurs somewhat an otherwise laudable opinion with a misreading of history. He maintains that peonage was neither a sectional nor a racial evil. How he arrived at this conclusion is not clear; perhaps the 1911 report of the Immigration Commission, which he quotes, misled him. There were some nonsouthern instances of peonage involving immigrants, just as Michigan and Minnesota had enacted (but never used) peonage laws. However, to draw from this skimpy list the conclusion that peonage was not traditionally both southern and racial is to fly in the face of the overwhelming mass of the evidence. Perhaps the interpretation arose from a desire to reassert concepts of national unity and downplay anything that might foment sectional disputes in time of war. One cannot tell, and perhaps it is petty to harp on what appears to be a side issue when the bulk of the opinion is of such high quality. However, the regional and racial nature was not only a part of the history of peonage, it was (and is) part of the problem in destroying it, and any solution that ignores or obscures this plain fact is likely to fail.

*Pollock* was the last peonage case to come before the Supreme Court, and it capped a brief period of significant federal interest in the practice. The CRS and the Supreme Court had created the legal instruments through which, it was felt, peonage could be destroyed. It was true that the slave-kidnapping statute had not yet been construed, but this was remedied in a 1947 circuit court decision. In *United States* v. *Ingalls*, slavery was defined as "enforced compulsory service to another"—as broad a definition as the Civil Rights Section could have asked.[23] (Further, as noted above, the revision of the *United States Code* had removed all the ambiguities in the language of the Anti-Peonage Act.)

With the end of the war, the new tools were permitted to rust. Although such organizations as the Workers Defense League continued to expose instances of peonage, few federal prosecutions resulted. In the early fifties a congressional investigation into labor conditions in Georgia disclosed that the law struck down in the *Taylor* case was still being used.[24] Perhaps more significantly, the Justice Department seems to have given up the ship. The 1961 Report of the United States Commission on Civil Rights notes that although there were sixty-seven complaints of peonage or slavery between 1958 and 1960, "no prosecutions were brought, apparently because none of those complaints was deemed valid." The department also reported evidence that the law declared unconstitutional in *Taylor* was still being used in Georgia, but again without recommendations for prosecution.[25] Harry H. Shapiro reviewed peonage complaints to the Justice Department from 1961 through 1963. Of a total of 104 complaints, only 2 resulted in prosecutions.[26]

When the *New Republic* published an article on peonage in Florida in 1969, the descriptions of the status of the peon could easily have been taken from reports in the days of the Black Codes.[27] Through the tumultuous sixties, in the teeth of the "civil rights revolution," peonage continued as before—perhaps reduced in magnitude by changing economic conditions, but still alive and kicking its victims as brutally as ever.

On the other hand, while there may be fewer peons in the South, the practice is spreading. It seems to have served best wherever the conditions of labor are worst. Thus Shapiro's statistics show an alarming rise in complaints from California, where, of course, the use of migrant Mexican laborers—a class easily open to exploitation—is more and more commonplace.

The inadequacy of the Justice Department in dealing with the problem is evident, and, despite all protestations to the contrary, one is led to doubt its good faith. To give the devil his due, however, good intentions and even vigorous investigations and prosecutions of complaints would not be likely to destroy the practice. As the Civil Rights Commission pointed out, "The victims of peonage and involuntary servitude are even less likely than the usual victims of police brutality and private violence to be articulate in protesting—especially if local officials cooperate with their 'masters.'"[28] One would like to see the department give it more of a try anyway; it is difficult to see who could lose by it, except the peon masters.

# Conclusion

*The natural operation of the statute . . . furnishes a convenient instrument for coercion . . . an instrument of compulsion particularly effective as against the poor and the ignorant, its most likely victim.*

Bailey v. Alabama *(1911)*

*. . . but no prosecutions were brought.*

Justice, *1962*

Perhaps the most striking aspect of the study of peonage is the boundless resilience of the institution. Created as a stopgap measure to reduce the effects of the abolition of slavery, it has survived all attempts to suppress it. Neither of the two great "civil rights revolutions"—Reconstruction and the post–*Brown* v. *Board* period of the late 1950s and 1960s—seems to have succeeded in producing changes. Indeed, there seems to have been little interest in doing so, to the degree that even the academic revolution in historiography fails to pay attention to the subject.[1] Considering the nature of the subject, its similarities to slavery, its brutality, and so forth, one is led continually to ask oneself, why? Why should a brutalizing and deceitful practice, which for much of its history held a majority of the black population of the South in thrall, be largely ignored by activist, reformer, and historian alike? Obviously no definitive answer to this question is possible. However, it seems appropriate at this point to make some conjectures on the subject.

Clearly the Reconstruction period is a key starting point—a jumping-off place for answers. This is true not only because it was in this period that the system got started, but also because this was probably the period in which it could most readily have been brought to a halt. Once peonage became firmly established and was allowed to flourish over a period of years, its capacity to endure was greatly enhanced. Once a practice, no matter how obnoxious, becomes a norm, its destruction is a formidable task. As in "legislating morality," the odds are against the innovator; inertia itself becomes a potent factor, and vast expenditures of energy are required.

In the chaos which was the South after the war, social change was clearly on the horizon. After the brief period of "presidential" Reconstruction, a righteous (and self-righteous) Congress interposed a significant federal presence into the area. The army and the Freedmen's Bureau did not do a perfect job, but they did produce some radical changes in the social system. The freedmen were sufficiently well protected in their civil rights that they were capable of casting votes, running for office, and being elected. In several states blacks made up about half of the state legislature. In short, while there were many setbacks, and the gains were often only temporary, the federal government succeeded to a degree in making over the political system of the South. As has been noted in the preceding chapters, however, that same government was a primary source of the coercion of Negro labor. Even the "radical" governments themselves were supportive of the practice, and although it is true that these legislatures were by no means really radical, they did take fairly strong action in such areas as voting rights and jury service. Why, alone among black rights, was the area of peonage never a matter of serious controversy?

No answer springs immediately to mind, but some conjectures seem more reasonable than others. First, the right to vote had (and has) great symbolic appeal. To Americans brought up on the litany of democracy and the Constitution, it is *the* vital question, the cornerstone of citizenship and freedom. To the degree that the Civil War was fought over the issue of slavery, the victors must have felt the need to ensure the full citizenship of the freed slave. The universal appeal of voting rights was, then, a strong argument for placing it first on the list. Additionally theorists, then and now, have argued that once you have the vote, all other civil rights flow naturally from it—that is, a group that can be a potent force in elections cannot be trifled with by its governors. This theory, while impressive on its face, is challenged by the events of the Reconstruction period, when the freedman did get the vote, but all the freed agricultural laborer got was peonage. Questions of jury service and equal treatment in the courts also provide an impressive repertoire of rhetoric— "equal justice under law," "a nation of laws," and so forth. These rights, too, are useful symbols of citizenship, easily defensible to all.

What then, of the right to be free from coercion in labor? A battle cry of "free labor" or "labor rights" would clearly have fallen flat in postbellum America. Once the onus of the word *slavery* is removed from the labor system, it might seem "radical" to push for true freedom of labor. The Black Codes, it is true, caused an uproar in the North, but they were openly discriminatory; and they were passed by the "unreconstructed legislatures" of the Old South, who were, after all, the "enemy." When the same system was imposed by the federal government or by the new legislatures (without open designations of color) they were accepted with ease.

It seems unwise, however, to place too much reliance on the symbolic aspect of the issue, for there was another major factor to distinguish peonage from other rights of freedmen. That is, of course, the factor of economics. The destruction of no other discriminatory system would cause the monetary losses that would occur upon the destruction of peonage. The South's economy was based on agriculture, and its agriculture was based on the plantation. The creation of a system of forced labor to replace slavery was the method least likely to disrupt that economy. The ex-slave had a contract and theoretically was paid wages; there was thus no overt basis for effective rhetoric, and the economics of agriculture could remain as undisturbed as possible in the circumstances.

Once the Reconstruction period is past, the prospects for the destruction of the practice are greatly lessened, for subsequent reform attempts must deal with new and difficult problems. Once the substitute for slavery had acquired the status of a social custom, enforcement of the antipeonage laws became extraordinarily tedious. A jury will be reluctant to convict a man on trial if many of his neighbors are equally guilty. In brief, the problems of enforcing those laws become similar to the problems faced by the enforcing of Prohibition laws.

In an article discussing the question of "legislating morality," John P. Roche and Milton M. Gordon set up a model by which the difficulties of taking effective action may be examined. Four areas of critical consideration are set up: the amount and geographical spread of opposition to the law, the intensity of opposition, the degree to which sanctions can be administered, and the diligence of enforcement.[2] (In the discussion below, I take some liberties with these criteria, and they form only a basic framework from which to carry on the discussion.)

In the first area, the geographical distribution of the opposition, peonage reform is subject to the same problems as any other civil rights activity in the South: the opposition is concentrated in those places where the violations are most numerous. At the turn of the century, for instance, peonage was widespread throughout the South, and while the opposition to change did not represent a majority of the nation, it did constitute an overwhelming percentage in that region. In later years, after economic changes had taken their toll of peonage, the opposition remained concentrated in those areas where peonage was still operating. Thus local government, juries, and law enforcement agencies were likely to be under opposition control.

To take a tack away from the Roche-Gordon position for a moment, the geographical question is also relevant in terms of the pro-reform forces, inasmuch as it may provide a partial answer to the lack of interest in peonage during the "civil rights revolution" of recent years. When civil rights leaders talk of voting rights, they appeal to a large constituency: all blacks are encompassed in the battle. Peonage, on the other hand, affects at this point only a fairly small percentage of the potential "support" community, and is thus less appealing as an issue.[3]

The intensity of the opposition also militates against effective reform. This is not true so much in the Roche-Gordon sense of the significance of "opinion-formers" (ministers, newspaper editors, etc.) as in the fact that what is being attacked is the opposition's pocketbook.[4] It is not ministers but plantation owners who oppose reform; not editors but turpentine camp operators. Few areas produce such vehement defenses as those made in behalf of one's livelihood. Not only will the opposition be intense in nature, but the successful peon master is likely to wield considerable economic power, even over the "opinion-makers."[5] (Further, this economic power is likely to affect the administration of justice; a sheriff who derives much of his income from a successful peonage operation in his district is unlikely to be eager to destroy the practice.)

The degree to which sanctions may be administered is one of the great stumbling blocks in enforcement of antipeonage legislation. Several highly significant factors come into play. First, the potential area of legal oversight is so diverse as to make effective enforcement extremely difficult. The voting rights enforcement provisions of the Civil Rights Act of 1965 probably represent the best example of a reasonably successful governmental intrusion for the protection of civil rights. When federal examiners were sent in to recalcitrant southern areas, the percentage of the black population registered to vote rose from 11.9 percent before their arrival, to 61.0 percent afterwards. The effect of the examiners' presence was so great that it had the effect of raising black registrations in adjoining nonexaminer areas (from 30.2 to 52.5 percent).[6] The marked success of this venture is striking; it is clearly the most effective action of its type ever taken by the federal government (and was almost instantaneous in that effect). However, this effort, massive as it was (fifteen hundred federal officials were active in the southern elections of 1966 and 1967), would be dwarfed by the force required to eradicate peonage effectively. Voting examiners have central locations to supervise, and these only at certain times. On the other hand, peonage may be taking place wherever one man employs another. The sheer size of the supervisory force necessary makes effective action highly unlikely, as long as the onus rests upon the federal government. The problem is akin to that facing the Department of Labor in enforcing wage-and-hour law provisions. In this case, however, there are no unions to assist, and violent retribution for those who might dare to complain is far more probable. In brief, the number and diversity of locations to be monitored militate against the efficient administration of the law.

The analogy just drawn relating to the enforcement of labor laws is perhaps appropriate in other ways—that is, the general difficulties in getting compliance with economic legislation may be relevant to the difficulties in the area of peonage. Laws that regulate some aspect of economic life are often felt to be less binding on the individual than other criminal laws.[7] Often the most vehement supporters of strict enforcement of laws against burglary or embezzlement will be forgiving to violators of trade practices regulations or wage-and-hour laws. There is far less social stigma attached to disobedience to the law in such cases. Violations of antipeonage laws would easily fall into this category except for one factor: that of violence. The intrusion of violence may make the peon master less acceptable to local society, and prosecutors tend to play up this factor whenever possible. Where evidence of violence is difficult to produce, as is often the case, it becomes difficult to get convictions. Clearly the racial element is significant here as well; as long as the justificatory rhetoric of the peon master is believed ("You can't get 'those people' to work unless you force them"), the social opprobrium for those who practice peonage will be slight. The idea of forcing lazy and re-calcitrant workers to perform useful labor is attractive: witness the consistent political appeal of "getting those welfare chiselers out on a job." It may be stretching the point to draw analogies between general labor legislation and antipeonage laws too closely, but a degree of similarity does exist.[8]

One additional factor that makes sanctions unlikely to be ad-ministered effectively relates to the inherent difficulties federal courts must face in areas like peonage. Given local levels of op-position, the main thrust against the practice must come from two areas of the federal structure—the Department of Justice and the courts. The courts have a variety of difficulties in this regard. First, they have no "self-starter" mechanism; they must rely on other parties to initiate action. Before the decision in *Wilson* v. *State* was appealed, for example, there was no way for its specious arguments to be dismissed. Secondly, certain areas of activity are relatively unsuitable for court control: for exam-ple, areas that require constant supervision and a continuous flow of information. There is a lack of control over all of the relevant parties to the particular problem along with a basic in-adequacy of "implementation procedures" beyond the instant case.[9] Federal courts have additional difficulties when state courts do not follow their lead; this recalcitrance is the classic check on higher-court power. In sum the federal courts, by themselves, are relatively helpless without a high degree of cooperation from the prosecutorial arm of the government.

This last statement brings us back to the last of the Roche-Gordon considerations—diligence of enforcement. The key point for diligent application of the law is seen to be in the "initial period when public attitudes . . . are in the process of formation."[10] Clearly, this criterion is not met; the Reconstruction era was the "initial period," and it was at this point that the government was espousing and enforcing peonage. In view of the difficulties in enforcing antipeonage laws after this period, only an extremely dedicated and consistent attack on the practice could have succeeded in making even a dent, let alone a breach, in its walls. It is difficult to see any real evidence of such a commitment. There were, certainly, especially in the two great periods of federal interest, many sincere and hardworking members of the Justice Department who were so committed. This was not the general trend, however, and indifference was far more common. The inadequacies of the Federal Bureau of Investigation in such areas has been widely discussed for many years; its record with regard to peonage does little to change such perceptions.

To conclude, the best chance for effective action on peonage was clearly at its inception. Failing that, the difficulties inherent in attacking an entrenched social custom would have required a massive and concerted effort in order to create change. In the atmosphere that existed, the efforts of those who were dedicated to the eradication of peonage were swallowed up, having only peripheral effects on the practice.

Neither the sins of capitalism nor the evil influence of racism can be seen as the whole answer to the dogged resilience of peonage. In the North, where racism was hardly unknown, the black laborer was not subjected to this sort of control. The South, at least as devoted to capitalism as the rest of the nation, rarely made peons of its white laboring force. Even that universally downtrodden and exploitable class, agricultural labor, was not so feudally bound to the land outside the South. Thus, black forced labor remained a legal and social construct specific to the southern situation, and clearly was as "peculiar" an institution as slavery itself.

Peonage clearly violates fundamental human rights. Its initial survival, under the aegis of law, was grotesque. Its continued occurrence, however sporadic and illegal, to the present time, reflects shamefully on the American system of justice.

# Notes

## Chapter 1

1. Theodore Wilson, *The Black Codes of the South* (Birmingham: University of Alabama Press, 1965), p. 63. Wilson's book is the only full study of the Black Codes, and as such, provided a jumping-off place for this section. A close reading of the statutes themselves, however, often belies Wilson's rather benign view of the legislatures. Ignoring his interpretations, it must be noted that his chronology is faultless, if his citations are not. While Wilson occasionally overlooks laws of significance to this study, or relevant sections of them, he provides a sound base of statutory citations on which to build.

2. Mississippi, *Laws*, 1865, c. 14.

3. See Labatt, *Master and Servant* (1913), 1:997–1007, and 10:8830–44, for a discussion of this subject; ibid., 1:997.

4. See, for example, the discussion of Chief Justice McIver in *State* v. *Aye*, S.C. 458 (1901); and Labatt, *Master and Servant*, 4:8067–94.

5. Mississippi, *Laws*, 1865, c. 17.

6. Ibid., c. 2.

7. Ibid., cc. 2, 46.

8. Mississippi, *Laws*, pp. 270–74. The reason given for failure to ratify was, in fact, that to do so would be tantamount to surrendering state sovereignty to Congress on purely intrastate matters.

9. See Wilson, *Black Codes*, pp. 70–71.

10. Vernon L. Wharton, *The Negro in Mississippi, 1865–1890* (Chapel Hill: North Carolina University Press, 1947), pp. 90–91.

11. Quoted in Wilson, *Black Codes*, p. 72.

12. South Carolina, *Laws*, 1865, c. 4.

13. Martin L. Abbott, *The Freedmen's Bureau in South Carolina, 1865–1872* (Chapel Hill: University of North Carolina Press, 1967), p. 73.

14. Louisiana, *Senate Journal*, 1865, p. 6.

15. It is unclear whether or not this particular act ever became law. It was certainly passed by the legislature, but it does not appear in this form in the *Acts* of 1865. John Engelsman, in "The Freedmen's Bureau in Louisiana," *Louisiana Historical Quarterly* 32 (1949):184, suggests that

the governor failed to sign it. Some portions are reflected in the other codes, particularly the vagrancy law. Perhaps it was not missed, as the bureau was doing the enforcement job in any case.

16. Louisiana, *Acts*, 1865, nos. 15–17.

17. See "Schurz Report" in U.S., Congress, *Senate Executive Documents*, 39th Cong., 1st sess., 1866, 2, p. 23; John and LaWanda Cox, "General O. O. Howard and the Misrepresented Bureau," *Journal of Southern History* 19 (1953):427.

18. Alabama, *Acts*, 1865–1866, nos. 107, 100, and 115. It is, of course, possible that the Alabama legislators anticipated the value of laws which were unbiased on their face, but whose application was understood by all. This is, obviously, sheer conjecture on my part.

19. Elizabeth Bethel, "Freedmen's Bureau in Alabama," *Journal of Southern History* 14 (1948) : 58.

20. Quoted in Wilson, *Black Codes*, p. 96.

21. Florida, *Acts*, 1866, cc. 1551, 1478.

22. Georgia, *Laws*, 1866, nos. 240, 217.

23. Ibid., no. 236. Wilson notes the first effect, but fails to discover the second. This kind of legal manipulation can be seen again in the actions of the Florida legislature in 1913 (see chapter 5, n. 44, below).

24. North Carolina, *Laws*, 1866, c. 42; Virginia, *Acts*, 1866, c. 15.

25. Texas, *Laws*, 1866, cc. 80, 82, 111, 120, and 63.

26. Arkansas, *Acts*, 1867.

27. Carter G. Woodson, *The Rural Negro* (Washington, D.C.: Association for the Study of Negro Life and History, 1930), p. 75.


*Chapter 2*


1. 13 *U.S. Statutes* 496.

2. John and LaWanda Cox, "General O. O. Howard and the Misrepresented Bureau," *Journal of Southern History* 19 (1953):427.

3. This consensus has been noted by James Sefton in *The U.S. Army and Reconstruction, 1865–1877* (Baton Rouge: Louisiana State University Press, 1967), p. 43, n. 49; and by Theodore Wilson, *The Black Codes of the South* (Birmingham: University of Alabama Press, 1965), chaps. 1 and 7, passim, but neither expands upon it to any great degree. William McFeely's *Yankee Stepfather* (New Haven, Conn.: Yale University Press, 1968) also deals with the issue, but it becomes somewhat obscured in his bitter denunciation of General Howard as a "stooge" for President Johnson and the planter class.

4. See, for example, orders of Generals Gordon (Va.), Herron (La.),

Slocum (Miss.), Canby (La.), quoted in Sefton, *U.S. Army*, pp. 42, 43, and passim; and U.S., Congress, *House Executive Documents*, 39th Cong., 1st sess., 1866, 70, pp. 23, 65, 66.

5. See, for example, the first portion of Chief Justice John Marshall's opinion in *Fletcher* v. *Peck* 6 Cranch 87 (1810); John P. Roche, "Entrepreneurial Liberty and the Fourteenth Amendment," *Labor History* 4 (1963): 3–10; Benjamin F. Wright, *The Contract Clause of the Constitution* (Cambridge, Mass.: Harvard University Press, 1938), passim; Edward S. Corwin, "The Basic Doctrine of American Constitutional Law," *Michigan Law Review* 12 (1914): 63–83.

6. See George R. Bentley, *A History of the Freedmen's Bureau* (Philadelphia: University of Pennsylvania Press, 1955), pp. 80–84; McFeely, *Yankee Stepfather*, chapter 8, passim.

7. Bentley, *Freedmen's Bureau*, pp. 80–81; see also John A. Carpenter, *Sword and Olive Branch: Oliver Otis Howard* (Pittsburgh, Pa.: University of Pittsburgh Press, 1964).

8. *House Executive Documents*, 39th Cong., 1st sess., 1866, 70, p. 263. This series of documents provides an accurate selection of bureau circulars, orders, and reports (see also ibid., 11, 19, 118, 120). Although not comprehensive the series has been commonly reproduced on microcards and represents a highly convenient source for bureau materials.

9. See Wilson, *Black Codes*, p. 58 and chapter 2, passim.

10. Vernon L. Wharton, *The Negro in Mississippi, 1865–1890* (Chapel Hill: University of North Carolina Press, 1947), pp. 90, 91; Sefton, *U.S. Army*, p. 71.

11. Martin L. Abbott, *The Freedmen's Bureau in South Carolina, 1865–1872* (Chapel Hill: University of North Carolina Press, 1967), p. 69 and chapter 5, passim.

12. Ibid., p. 73; Wilson, *Black Codes*, pp. 75, 83.

13. Quoted in Wilson, *Black Codes*, p. 84. See also Abbott, *Freedmen's Bureau*, p. 73. Abbott, whether by design or not, describes Sickles's and Scott's orders as requiring that the disobedient will be "removed from the land"—he makes no mention of arrests for vagrancy or the hiring out of labor. Wilson, on the other hand, describes Sickles as a representative of the bureau. This latter error is more understandable, however, as officials of both the army and the bureau held military titles. Both organizations, in fact, seem to have been staffed exclusively by generals, and a modern observer is led to wonder if their efficiency might not have been increased dramatically by the inclusion of a private or two to carry out orders.

14. From General Order no. 12, quoted in Elizabeth Bethel, "The

Freedmen's Bureau in Alabama," *Journal of Southern History* 14 (1948):54–55, 57.

15. *House Executive Documents*, 39th Cong., 1st sess., 1866, 30, p. 13. See also Bethel, "Freedmen's Bureau in Alabama," pp. 57–58; and Wilson, *Black Codes*, pp. 59, 76.

16. Bethel, "Freedmen's Bureau in Alabama," pp. 52–55.

17. Bentley, *Freedmen's Bureau*, pp. 23, 58.

18. Charles Kassel, "The Labor System of General Banks—A Lost Episode of Civil War History," *Open Court* 43 (1928):41–45. See also McFeely, *Yankee Stepfather*, pp. 170–71, for a bitter denunciation of Banks, and John C. Engelsman, "The Freedmen's Bureau in Louisiana," *Louisiana Historical Quarterly* 32 (1944):175–76.

19. Engelsman, "Freedmen's Bureau in Louisiana," p. 176.

20. Ibid., pp. 178, 171; "Schurz Report" in U.S., Congress, *Senate Executive Documents*, 39th Cong., 1st sess., 1866, 2, pp. 90–92; McFeely, *Yankee Stepfather*, pp. 171–72; *House Executive Documents*, 39th Cong., 1st sess., 1866, 70, p. 18.

21. Bentley, *Freedmen's Bureau*, pp. 70, 71, 107–9; McFeely, *Yankee Stepfather*, p. 178.

22. Engelsman, "Freedmen's Bureau in Louisiana," pp. 178–87, 217; see also McFeely, *Yankee Stepfather*, pp. 179–80.

23. Georgia, *Laws*, 1866, no. 195; *House Executive Documents*, 39th Cong., 1st sess., 1866, 70, p. 65.

24. Sefton, *U.S. Army*, p. 71; Wilson, *Black Codes*, p. 84.

25. Quoted in Wilson, *Black Codes*, p. 84. (The problems inherent in dealing with laws nondiscriminatory on their face are made clear in this case. Terry was somewhat embarrassed by the revelation that the Virginia legislature had copied its law from the Pennsylvania statute then in force. He was undoubtedly correct as to the intent and probable application of the law, but the congressional conservatives enjoyed the anomaly.) See U.S., Congress, *Congressional Globe*, 39th Cong., 1st sess., pt. 1, p. 603.

26. Quoted in Wilson, *Black Codes*, pp. 83–84; Bentley, *Freedmen's Bureau*, p. 84.

27. Bentley, *Freedmen's Bureau*, pp. 84, 155–56; see Joe M. Richardson, "The Freedmen's Bureau and Negro Labor in Florida" and "Evaluation of the Freedmen's Bureau in Florida," *Florida Historical Quarterly* 39 (1960) and 41 (1963).

28. Charles Ramsdell, *Reconstruction in Texas* (New York: Longmans, Green, 1910), p. 101; quoted in McFeely, *Yankee Stepfather*, p. 153; Bentley, *Freedmen's Bureau*, p. 149; order quoted in McFeely, *Yankee Stepfather*, p. 154.

29. It is fascinating to note that McFeely, a revisionist, draws his newspaper quotations almost exclusively from the radical *New Orleans Tribune*, while Engelsman relies totally on the *New Orleans Times, Daily Picayune*, and *Price-Current*. The situation in Louisiana is gone into in somewhat greater detail as it provides the basis of McFeely's denunciations.

30. See, for example, the facts of the case in *Lee* v. *West* 47 Ga. 312, where bureau agents removed black laborers from a jail to which they had been brought by a planter and his "heavies."

31. Bentley, *Freedmen's Bureau*, chapters 8–10, passim.

### Chapter 3

1. See, for example, the conclusions in the *Report of the Commissioner of Agriculture for the Year 1867* (Washington, D.C., 1868), pp. 412–28, describing production in the South despite disastrous weather and the introduction of the new systems of labor. Wages, it should be noted, had dropped significantly between 1867 and 1868.

2. Louisiana, *Acts*, 1869, no. 28; see above, chapter 1, n. 15.

3. Sheppard's indexes to cases and statutes, for instance, relied on with fundamentalist faith by the modern legal scholar, are almost totally useless for this period. Further, the state codes often fail to list statutes seemingly enacted and signed.

4. South Carolina, *Acts*, 1869, sec. 4, p. 227. This act is quoted, among others, in full in LaWanda Cox and John Cox, eds., *Reconstruction, the Negro, and the New South* (Columbia: University of South Carolina Press, 1973), as an example of the comparatively radical makeup of the South Carolina legislature.

5. This portion of the statute was declared unconstitutional in *State* v. *Williams* 32 S.C. 123 in 1890, in a decision based on the discrimination in punishment. However, as the legislature had conveniently amended the statute in 1889, equalizing the penalties, the new statute took effect without any disruption of the system.

6. George R. Bentley, *A History of the Freedmen's Bureau* (Philadelphia: University of Pennsylvania Press, 1955), p. 159.

7. C. Vann Woodward, *Origins of the New South* (Baton Rouge: Louisiana State University Press, 1951), p. 180.

8. South Carolina, *Revised Statutes*, 1873, pp. 557–58; South Carolina, 15 *Statutes at Large* 884.

9. South Carolina, *Revised Statutes*, 1873, p. 433.

10. See *Century Digest*, "Statute of Frauds," vol. 23–24, sec. 5, nos.

68–75, passim, for a review of all reported cases throughout the nation on the subject.

11. *Hair* v. *Blease* 8 S.C. 63 (1876); *Daniel* v. *Swearengen* 6 S.C. 297 (1875).

12. See the history of the statutes given by Justice McGowan in *Carpenter* v. *Strickland* 20 S.C. 1 (1833); also *Huff* v. *Watkins* 15 S.C. 82 (1881), and *Kennedy* v. *Reames* 15 S.C. 548 (1881).

13. *Daniel* v. *Swearengen* 6 S.C. 297, 300 (1875).

14. Mississippi, *Laws*, 1870, pp. 73, 95, 374–75.

15. Mississippi, *Revised Code*, 1871, sec. 2836.

16. Vernon L. Wharton, *The Negro in Mississippi, 1865–1890* (Chapel Hill: University of North Carolina Press, 1947), pp. 94–95.

17. Ibid., p. 95.

18. Mississippi, *Digest of Cases*.

19. Wharton, *Negro in Mississippi*, p. 238.

20. Mississippi, *Laws*, 1872, pp. 67–86; ibid., 1875, pp. 107–8.

21. Ibid., p. 107.

22. Mississippi, *Laws*, 1867, p. 569; ibid., 1872, p. 131.

23. See opinion in *Doty* v. *Heath* 52 Miss. 530 (1876); *Betts* v. *Ratliff* 50 Miss. 561 (1874); Mississippi, *Laws*, 1873, p. 79.

24. See *Betts* v. *Ratliff* 50 Miss. 561 (1874), *Cayce* v. *Stovall* 50 Miss. 396 (1874), and *Arbuckle* v. *Nelms* 50 Miss. 556 (1874).

25. *Buck* v. *Payne* 52 Miss. 271–73 (1876).

26. *Kerr* v. *Moore* 54 Miss. 286 (1876).

27. Alabama, *Laws*, 1866–1867, p. 504. See, for example, *Boulo* v. *State* 49 Ala. 22 (1873). Elizabeth Bethel, in "The Freedmen's Bureau in Alabama," *Journal of Southern History* 14 (1948), for example, claims that the legislature repealed the law because of adverse reaction to it (p. 67).

28. See *Colly* v. *State* 55 Ala. 85 (1876) and *Sandy* v. *State* 60 Ala. 58 (1877).

29. 44 Ala. 367 (1870).

30. See Labatt, *Master and Servant* (1913), 4:8068, for this interpretation. See also, *Turner* v. *State* 48 Ala. 549 (1872) and *Roseberry* v. *State* 50 Ala. 160 (1874).

31. Alabama, *Laws*, 1868, p. 365; ibid., 1872, p. 78.

32. Alabama, *Laws*, 1868, pp. 455–56; ibid., 1871, p. 19; *Gafford* v. *Stearns* 51 Ala. 434 (1874).

33. Howard A. White, *The Freedmen's Bureau in Louisiana* (Baton Rouge: Louisiana State University Press, 1970), p. 122; Louisiana, *Laws*, 1868, no. 97.

34. *State* v. *J. H. Sypher* and *J. L. Petit* 19 La. Ann. 71 (1867). This case

also provided one of those charming coincidences which lighten a re-searcher's task. Mr. Sypher, one of the defendants in this case, appar-ently also supplied himself with freedmen by outright kidnapping by his band of overseers. He was also charged with jumping bail (see the facts in the case). I came across his name again in Ella Lonn, *Reconstruc-tion in Louisiana* (New York: Putnam, 1918), p. 346. Professor Lonn, an ardent "Dunningite," was describing the outrageous conduct of the freedmen during Reconstruction. White women, it appears, were afraid to go out without a pistol. "They dared not leave the plantation," and at night one could hear the horses resist when the Negroes borrowed them for joyrides. Only when the lynching of a black in the township "had a salutary effect" was order restored. The helpless victim of these gross misdeeds (which also included the theft of salt from saltshakers and buttons from clothing) was none other than Mrs. J. H. Sypher. Perhaps if Mr. Sypher had spent less time on the road capturing la-borers, his gang of overseers could have controlled this sort of black revelry.

35. See *Moore* v. *Gray* 22 La. Ann. 289 (1870).

36. See *Bryan* v. *State* 44 Ga. 328 (1871) and *Wharton* v. *Jossey* 46 Ga. 578 (1872).

37. *Hodgins* v. *State* 126 Ga. 639 (1906) at 640–41.

38. See the facts in *Lee* v. *West* 47 Ga. 312–15 (1872).

39. Ibid., pp. 317–18 (emphasis added). The judge goes on to ex-coriate the bureau for interfering in the matter.

40. *Ryan* v. *State* 45 Ga. 128 (1872).

41. *Ratteree* v. *State* 77 Ga. 774. This attempt was also foiled by the court, and as a result the Georgia legislature promptly passed a con-tract law. See history in *Lamar* v. *State* 120 Ga. 312.

42. A. F. McKelway, "The Convict Lease System of Georgia," *Outlook* 90 (1908):68.

43. Georgia, *Laws*, 1874, p. 29 (title 6, no. 25).

44. See *Alexander* v. *Glenn* 39 Ga. 1 (1869), *Saulsbury* v. *Eason* 47 Ga. 617 (1872); Georgia, *Revised Code*, 1873, sec. 1978; Georgia, *Laws*, 1875, p. 20 (title 4, no. 18).

45. *State* v. *Custer* 65 N.C. 311 (1871).

46. *Haskins* v. *Royster* 70 N.C. 481 (1874) (emphasis in the original); see opinion in *State* v. *Shaft* 78 N.C. 464.

47. See, for example, *Hunt* v. *Wing* 57 Tenn. (10 Heisk.) 139 (1872) and *Lewis* v. *Mahon* 68 Tenn. (9 Baxt.) 374 (1878) on liens; see also the enticement law in Tennessee, *Acts*, 1875, p. 168; *Taylor* v. *Hathaway* 29 Ark. 597 (1874); *Burgie* v. *Davis* 34 Ark. 179 (1879) and *Alexander* v.

*Pardue* 30 Ark. 359 (1875); *Ruffin* v. *Commonwealth* 21 Grat. (Va.) 790 (1871); *Ex parte Stubblefield* 1 Tex. App. 757 (1877) for a sampling of cases and statutes of the period.

## Chapter 4

1. South Carolina, 16 *Statutes at Large* 265, 410, 713, 743; *Columbia Daily Register*, December 5, 1877, quoted in George B. Tindall, *South Carolina Negroes, 1877–1900* (New York: Columbia University Press, 1952), p. 109.

2. Quoted in C. Vann Woodward, *Origins of the New South* (Baton Rouge: Louisiana State University Press, 1951), p. 180.

3. Ibid., p. 181.

4. Almost all breach of contract, parol contract, and parol lien cases reported in the period deal with "colored men," "negroes," or "darkies," and, to repeat, only those cases carried to appellate court are reported.

5. See Oscar Zeichner, "The Transition of Slave to Free Agricultural Labor in the Southern States," *Agricultural History* 13 (1939): 22–32; *Report of the Commissioner of Agriculture*, (1867), p. 417; U.S., Census Office, Tenth Census, 1880, *Report on Cotton Production in the United States*, 6:61; Tindall, *South Carolina Negroes*, p. 106.

6. Some states had no penitentiary tradition, having largely relied on county systems in which corporal punishment (whipping, stocks, etc.) had been the rule. See Blake McKelvey, "Penal Slavery and Southern Reconstruction," *Journal of Negro History* 20 (1935): 154–55.

7. Ibid., pp. 156–60.

8. George Washington Cable, *The Silent South together with the Freedman's Case in Equity and the Convict Lease System* (New York: Scribner's, 1889), p. 152.

9. Georgia, *Laws*, 1875, p. 26 (title 4, no. 29); Mississippi, *Revised Code*, 1880, sec. 2901.

10. Vernon L. Wharton, *The Negro in Mississippi, 1865–1890* (Chapel Hill: University of North Carolina Press, 1947), p. 239; *Second Annual Report of the Commissioner of Labor, 1866: Convict Labor* (Washington, D.C., 1877), pp. 300–303; Tillman quoted in Tindall, *South Carolina Negroes*, p. 267.

11. Wharton, *Negro in Mississippi*, p. 235; Alabama, *Laws*, 1882, sec. 5, p. 134.

12. Louisiana, *Revised Laws*, 1884, sec. 2862; North Carolina, *Revised Code*, 1883, sec. 3422; Mississippi, *Acts*, 1882, c. 40, sec. 3; South

Carolina, *Revised Statutes*, 1882, sec. 2729; Tennessee, *Revised Code*, 1884, sec. 6367.

13. See J. C. Powell, *The American Siberia; or, Fourteen Years' Experience in a Southern Convict Camp* (Chicago: H. J. Smith, 1891), p. 332. (Powell was the warden of Florida's lease camp system.)

14. C. Vann Woodward, *Tom Watson; Agrarian Rebel* (New York: Macmillan, 1938), p. 25; U.S., Congress, *Congressional Record*, 47th Cong., 2d sess., 1883, 14, p. 2493; Tindall, *South Carolina Negroes*, p. 271.

15. Woodward, *Origins*, p. 214.

16. *Convict Labor*, pp. 300, 301, 303, 323.

17. Woodward, *Origins*, p. 215.

18. McKelvey, "Penal Slavery," p. 160.

19. See Dan T. Carter, "Prisons, Politics and Business: The Convict Lease System in the Post–Civil War South" (M.A. thesis, University of Wisconsin, 1964), p. 95. This is an excellent bibliographical source for materials on convict leasing, but it is confused chronologically and fails to consider the laws upon which the system was based.

20. *Convict Labor*, p. 507.

21. Arkansas, *Revised Statutes*, 1884, secs. 1213, 1214, 1235; Florida, *Laws*, 1881, c. 47, sec. 5; Georgia, *Revised Code*, 1882, secs. 4814, 4821 a,b,c; Mississippi, *Revised Code*, 1880, secs. 3174, 3175; North Carolina, *Revised Code*, 1883, sec. 3448; Tennessee, *Revised Code*, 1884, secs. 6275, 6284; Texas, *Revised Statutes*, 1879, arts. 3602, 3603, 3604; Virginia, *Acts*, 1878, c. 39, sec. 19 (these laws are listed because no other such compilation was discovered by this writer in any work on the subject); Louisiana, *Revised Laws*, 1897, p. 666, secs. 7, 8 (the act was passed in 1894); Alabama, *Revised Code*, 1897, sec. 4532 (the act was passed in 1882).

22. Ray Stannard Baker, *Following the Color Line* (New York: Doubleday, 1908), pp. 96–97.

23. Clarissa Olds Keeler, *The Crime of Crimes; or, The Convict System Unmasked* (Washington, D.C.: Pentecostal Era Co., 1907), pp. 7–12.

24. Charles W. Russell, *Report on Peonage* (Washington, D.C.: U.S. Department of Justice, 1908), p. 26.

25. Richard B. Morris, "The Course of Peonage in a Slave State," *Political Science Quarterly* 65 (1950):239 and "Labor Controls in Maryland in the Nineteenth Century," *Journal of Southern History* 14 (1948):385.

26. An excellent history of the system is given in the opinion in *Jaremillo* v. *Romero* 1 N.M. 190 (1857), in which the case was dismissed, but only on the grounds that the *debt* was not proven.

27. See *Wood* v. *Hookina* 3 Haw. 102 (1869); *Wood* v. *Afo* 3 Haw. 444 (1873); *Hilo Sugar Co.* v. *Mioshi* 8 Haw. 201 (1891); see also *Rickard* v. *Couto* 5 Haw. 507 (1885); *Laupahoehoe Sugar Co.* v. *Kanaele* 9 Haw. 468 (1894). A decent, if biased, description of the system is given in Katherine Coman, *The History of Contract Labor in the Hawaiian Islands* (New York: Macmillan, 1903). A similar system existed in the Philippines after the Spanish-American War, and for many years afterwards. See Dean C. Worcester, *Report on Slavery and Peonage in the Philippine Islands* (Washington, D.C.: Bureau of Printing, 1913).

28. Alabama, *Revised Code*, 1896, c. 154, sec. 4730; Arkansas, *Laws*, 1894, c. 78, sec. 4790; Florida, *Laws*, 1891, c. 4032; Georgia, *Acts*, 1903, no. 345, p. 90; Louisiana, *Acts*, 1892, no. 50, p. 516, sec. 1; Mississippi, *Acts*, 1900, c. 101, sec. 1; North Carolina, *Revised Code*, 1883, c. 33, secs. 3119, 3120; South Carolina, *Revised Code*, 1902, c. 16, sec. 357; Tennessee, *Revised Code*, 1884, sec. 3438.

29. See, for example, Labatt, *Master and Servant* (1913), 7:320; or Lafayette M. Hershaw, "Peonage," *Occasional Papers of the American Negro Academy* 15 (1915). Labatt, in the standard work in the period on the subject of master-servant relationships in law, omits Arkansas, Mississippi, and Tennessee from his discussion.

30. Georgia, *Acts*, 1903, no. 345, p. 90.

31. *Brown* v. *State* 8 Ga. App. 211 (1910).

32. *Young* v. *State* 4 Ga. App. 827 (1908).

33. *Lamar* v. *State* 120 Ga. 312 (1904); *Banks* v. *State* 124 Ga. 15 (1905); *Townsend* v. *State* 124 Ga. 69 (1905); *Brown* v. *State* 8 Ga. App. 211 (1910).

34. *Vance* v. *State* 128 Ga. 661 (1907).

35. *State* v. *Williams* 32 S.C. 123 (1890).

36. See, for example, *Ex parte Riley* 94 Ala. 82 (1891); *McIntosh* v. *State* 117 Ala. 128 (1897); *Copeland* v. *State* 97 Ala. 30 (1893); *Thomson* v. *State* 56 Fla. 107 (1908); *State* v. *Murray* 116 La. 655 (1906); *State* v. *Norman* 110 N.C. 484 (1892); *State* v. *Leak* 62 S.C. 405 (1901).

37. See the body of the statutes referred to in n. 28, above.

38. *State* v. *Williams* 32 S.C. 123 (1890).

39. Alabama, *Revised Code*, 1897, c. 192, secs. 5504, 5505, 5506, 5509; Arkansas, *Laws*, 1894, c. 78, sec. 4792; Florida, *Revised Statutes*, 1891, sec. 2405; Georgia, *Revised Code*, 1895, secs. 121, 122; Louisiana, *Acts*, 1892, no. 50, p. 516, sec. 2; Mississippi, *Revised Code*, 1892, c. 29, sec. 1068; North Carolina, *Revised Code*, 1893, c. 33, secs. 3119, 3120; South Carolina, *Revised Code*, 1902, c. 16, sec. 359; Tennessee, *Revised Code*, 1884, secs. 3438, 3439. N.B.: North Carolina and Tennessee combined the offenses of enticement and breach under the same title.

40. Florida, *Revised Statutes*, 1891, sec. 2405.

41. *Bryan* v. *State* 44 Ga. 328 (1871); *McBride* v. *O'Neal* 128 Ga. 473 (1907).

42. *Hudgins* v. *State* 126 Ga. 630 (1906); *Kine* v. *Eubanks* 109 La. 242. ("This is a matter of common knowledge": *Wolf* v. *New Orleans Tailor-Made Pants Co.* 113 La. 388 [1904].) See also *State* v. *Harwood* 104 N.C. 724 (1889).

43. Georgia, *Revised Code*, 1895, see secs. 121 and 122; Miller quoted in Tindall, *South Carolina Negroes*, p. 112.

44. Alabama, *Revised Code*, 1907, sec. 6851; 44 Ala. 368 (1871); see controlling cases listed in *Tenth Special Report of the Commissioner of Labor: Labor Laws of the United States* (Washington: Bureau of Printing, 1904), p. 108.

45. See, for example, *Armistead* v. *Chatters* 71 Miss. 509 (1893); *Hoole* v. *Dorroh* 75 Miss. 257 (1897); *Tarpley* v. *State* 79 Ala. 271 (1885); *Driscoll* v. *State* 77 Ala. 84 (1884); *State* v. *West* 106 La. 274 (1902); *State* v. *Harwood* 104 N.C. 724 (1889); *Duckett* v. *Pool* 34 S.C. 311 (1890); *Tucker* v. *State* 86 Ark. 436 (1908).

46. E.g., *Armistead* v. *Chatters* 71 Miss. 509 (1893); *Tarpley* v. *State* 79 Ala. 271 (1885); *Sturdivant* v. *Tolette* 84 Ark. 412 (1907).

47. *Armistead* v. *Chatters* 71 Miss. 509.

48. 322 U.S. 4. "This is not to intimate that this section, more than others, was sympathetic with peonage ... for this evil ... and its sporadic appearances have been neither sectional nor racial."

49. *Bourlier Bros.* v. *Macauley* 91 Ky. 135 (1891); Michigan, *Laws*, 1903, no. 106, sec. 2; Minnesota, *Revised Laws*, 1905, sec. 5178.

50. Leftist works on the subject took the line that almost all workers in capitalistic America were peons. See, for example, Walter Wilson, *Forced Labor in the United States* (New York: International Publishers, 1933).

51. Woodward, *Tom Watson*, p. 220.

52. Harold U. Faulkner, *Politics, Reform and Expansion* (New York: Harper and Row, 1959), p. 270. Quoted in Herbert Shapiro, "The Populists and the Negro," in August Meier and Elliot Rudwick, eds., *The Making of Black America* (New York: Atheneum, 1969), 2:33.

53. Richard Hofstadter, *The Age of Reform* (New York: Knopf, 1955), p. 61; Woodward, *Origins*, pp. 258, 257.

54. Woodward, *Tom Watson*, p. 218; *Origins*, p. 205.

55. Woodward, *Tom Watson*, p. 219.

56. *Convict Labor*, pp. 303, 300, 301. (See also, quotations on convict labor section, pp. 33, 34.)

57. Even here, the Populists opposed the "Force Bill" which would

have introduced a federal presence to protect black suffrage in the South. The Negro Alliances supported it overwhelmingly, but the white Populists stood foursquare for "home rule" and "states' rights." See Shapiro, "Populists and the Negro," p. 33.

58. Dunbar, quoted in Shapiro, "Populists and the Negro," p. 32.

*Chapter 5*

1. It is true that a federal court had overturned a Maryland apprenticeship law in 1867 as violating the Civil Rights Act of 1866, but the case never reached the Supreme Court. (It was generally considered that the passage of the Fourteenth Amendment had made an appeal useless.) *Matter of Turner* 1 Abb. (U.S.) 84 (1867).

2. 92 U.S. 542 (1876), 109 U.S. 3 (1883), and 106 U.S. 629 (1883).

3. 14 U.S. *Statutes* 546 (now sec. 158 of the *United States Code*). Senators Trumbull and Sumner, the major sponsors of the bill, believed that the Slave Kidnapping and Civil Rights Act of 1866 probably covered peonage, but they decided to support this additional legislation to cover all contingencies. (The Slave Kidnapping Act was revived for such use in 1939—see chapter 7.) Howard Devon Hamilton, "The Legislative and Judicial History of the Thirteenth Amendment" (Ph.D. diss., University of Illinois, 1950), pp. 171–72. This work gives an excellent summary of the legislative history of the congressional enactments which were used to prosecute those who held peons.

4. 14 U.S. *Statutes* 546, sec. 1. When the act was recodified in 1948, the specific references to New Mexico were deleted, without other significant changes.

5. Ray Stannard Baker, *Following the Color Line* (New York: Doubleday, 1908); Charles W. Russell, *Report on Peonage* (Washington: U.S. Department of Justice, 1908); U.S., Congress, *Reports of the U.S. Immigration Commission*, Senate Documents 747, 61st Cong., 3d sess., 1911; *Report of the Attorney General of the United States*, 1907, exhibit 17, p. 211.

6. *U.S.* v. *Eberhardt* 127 Fed. 252 (Ga. 1899).

7. C. Vann Woodward, *Origins of the New South* (Baton Rouge: Louisiana State University Press, 1951), pp. 262, 339.

8. Pete Daniel, *The Shadow of Slavery: Peonage in the South, 1901–1969* (Urbana: University of Illinois Press, 1972), p. 44.

9. *Peonage Cases* 123 Fed. 671 (Ala. 1903). This charge and the one in the Florida case were reprinted in the *Federal Reporter* and were prime sources of definitions for future prosecutions.

10. Ibid.

11. Ibid.

12. See William W. Howe, "The Peonage Cases," *Columbia Law Review* 4 (1904):285.

13. *Clyatt* v. *United States* 197 U.S. 201 (1905). There is no report of the charge to the grand jury in *United States* v. *Clyatt* and there does not seem to be much in the way of interpretation evident from the trial record found in the Supreme Court transcript of record. Therefore, although this was the first reported case under the statute, it did not become significant until it reached the Supreme Court; see comments of District Judge Swayne, *In re Peonage Charge*, 138 Fed. 686 (Fla. 1905), in his charge to the grand jury.

14. 197 U.S. 207 (1905). The statute, it may be recalled, made it a crime to "hold, arrest or return . . . persons to a condition of peonage." 14 U.S. *Statutes* 546, sec. 1.

15. 14 U.S. *Statutes* 546, sec. 2.

16. See, for example, *Civil Rights Cases* 109 U.S. 3 (1883).

17. *Clyatt* v. *United States*, 197 U.S. 207 (1905).

18. Ibid.

19. Ibid.; Brewer was here quoting from the New Mexico case referred to earlier, *Jaremillo* v. *Romero*, 1 N.M. 194 (1857).

20. See the case notes of the period, e.g., "Peonage" in *Columbia Law Review* 8 (1908):318–19; ibid., 11 (1911):365; *Harvard Law Review* 21 (1908):628; *Michigan Law Review* 6 (1908):504–5; *Pennsylvania Law Review* 55 (1907):508–9; ibid., 57 (1908):464–68.

21. *Clyatt* v. *United States* 197 U.S. 207 (1905).

22. Daniel, *Shadow of Slavery*, p. 17.

23. 219 U.S. 219 (1911).

24. *Clyatt* v. *United States* 197 U.S. 207 (1905); *In re Peonage Charge* 138 Fed. 686 (Fla. 1905).

25. *Peonage Cases* 123 Fed. 671 (Ala. 1903).

26. *In re Peonage Charge* 138 Fed. 686 (Fla. 1905).

27. Ibid.

28. *United States* v. *Clement* 171 Fed. 974 (S.C. 1909).

29. *Clyatt* v. *United States* 197 U.S. 207 (1905); *United States* v. *Clement* 171 Fed. 974 (S.C. 1909). Indeed, they are also subject to prosecution under all that remained of the Civil Rights Enforcement Act of 1870, which provided for the prosecution of any official who, under "color of law" deprives any person of his civil rights. (See the discussion in chapter 7.)

30. *United States* v. *Clement* 171 Fed. 974 (S.C. 1909); *In re Peonage Charge* 138 Fed. 686 (Fla. 1905).

31. *In re Peonage Charge* 138 Fed. 686 (Fla. 1905).

32. See, for example, *State* v. *Vann* 150 Ala. 66 (1907), and cases listed in chapter 4.

33. New York, *Revised Code*, 1882, sec. 673. See, for example, *State* v. *Murray* 116 La. 655 (1906), in which Justice Breaux quotes the New York statute and a similar New Jersey law as the basis for his decision upholding the Louisiana act.

34. Freund, *The Police Power, Public Policy, and Constitutional Rights* (Chicago: Callaghan, 1904), sec. 452; *State* v. *Murray* 116 La. 655 (1906).

35. 197 U.S. 221. The Supreme Court in *Adair* v. *United States* 208 U.S. 161 (1908) had also noted "It may be—but upon that point we express no opinion—that in the case of a labor contract between an employer engaged in interstate commerce and his employee, Congress could make it a crime for either party without sufficient or just excuse or notice to disregard the terms of such contract or to refuse to perform it." This was also used to defend the state's position, even by legal authorities. Labatt, *Master and Servant* (1913), sec. 2832, n. 2.

36. *Ex parte Hollman* 79 S.C. 9 (1907).

37. *Peonage Cases* 123 Fed. 671 (Ala. 1903).

38. *Robertson* v. *Baldwin* 165 U.S. 275 (1897).

39. See *Turner's Case* 24 Fed. Cas. no. 14, 248 (1825).

40. *Robertson* v. *Baldwin* 165 U.S. 275 (1897).

41. Ibid.; 30 U.S. *Statutes* 755 (1898). See Hamilton, "Legislative History," p. 143. The passage of the La Follette Merchant Seaman Act in 1915 finally ended the controversy, as a result of years of efforts by Andrew Furuseth, head of the Seaman's Union, and Victor Olander, his vice-president.

42. See chapter 4, nn. 30–34, 36, 45, for some of these cases.

43. *Ex parte Drayton* 153 Fed. 986 (S.C. 1907); *Ex parte Hollman* 79 S.C. 9 (1908).

44. Florida, *Laws*, 1891, c. 4032; *Laws*, 1907, c. 5678.

45. *Toney* v. *State* 141 Ala. 120 (1904) following Jones's declaration of unconstitutionality in *Peonage Cases* 123 Fed. 271 (Ala. 1903).

46. 219 U.S. 219 (1911).

47. See, for example, *Glenn* v. *State* 123 Ga. 585 (1905); *State* v. *Norman* 110 N.C. 484 (1892); *State* v. *Robinson* 70 S.C. 468 (1905); *Saunders* v. *State* 7 Ga. App. 46 (1909); *James* v. *State* 5 Ga. App. 353 (1908); *Starling* v. *State* 5 Ga. App. 171 (1908); *State* v. *Griffin* 154 N.C. 611 (1911); *State* v. *Leak* 62 S.C. 405 (1901).

48. *Bailey* v. *State* 158 Ala. 18 (1908).

49. Alabama, *Revised Code*, 1907, sec. 6845; Florida, *Statutes at Large*, 1906, sec. 3320; Georgia, *Acts*, 1903, no. 345, sec. 2; North Carolina, *Revised Code*, 1905, sec. 3431; Mississippi, *Revised Code*, 1906, sec. 1148;

South Carolina, *Revised Code*, 1912, secs. 492, 494.

50. *Ex parte Riley* 94 Ala. 82 (1891); *Dorsey* v. *State* 111 Ala. 40 (1895); *McIntosh* v. *State* 117 Ala. 128 (1897); see also, *Copeland* v. *State* 97 Ala. 30 (1893); and *Tennyson* v. *State* 97 Ala. 78 (1893).

51. For an excellent and full description of some progressive Alabamians' efforts to get a test case to the Court, and the results of their success (loss of elective offices, etc.), see Pete Daniel, "Up from Slavery and Down to Peonage: The Alonzo Bailey Case," *Journal of American History* 51 (1970):654–70.

52. See the facts in *Bailey* v. *Alabama* 219 U.S. 219 (1911). Thomas released Bailey, after a preliminary trial, on a writ of habeas corpus, which was reversed by a higher court. See *Bailey* v. *State* 158 Ala. 15 (1908). Thomas subsequently lost his position as a result. See Daniel, *Shadow of Slavery*, chapter 4, passim.

53. *Bailey* v. *Alabama* 219 U.S. 219 (1911). In *Hodges* v. *United States* 203 U.S. 1 (1906) the Court had overturned the conviction for peonage of a group of "whitecappers," who had, by violence, prevented some blacks from fulfilling their contracts. "No mere personal assault . . . operates to reduce the individual to a condition of slavery." Thus the Thirteenth Amendment did not permit the application of the Civil Rights Acts, and the Fourteenth could not reach private action. The widespread extent and discrimination of this practice of "whitecapping" was ignored. This is also one of the few cases in which the right to contract freely was not upheld by the Supreme Court. Harlan, of course, dissented.

54. *Ex parte Riley* 94 Ala. 82 (1891); *Bailey* v. *Alabama* 219 U.S. 219 (1911); *Bailey* v. *State* 161 Ala. 75 (1910) (petition for rehearing).

55. *Bailey* v. *Alabama* 219 U.S. 219 (1911).

56. Ibid.

57. Ibid.

58. See Samuel J. Konefsky, *The Legacy of Holmes and Brandeis* (New York: Macmillan, 1956), chapters 1 and 2, passim; Max Lerner, *The Mind and Faith of Justice Holmes* (New York: Halcyon, 1943), p. 148 and passim.

59. *United States* v. *Reynolds* 235 U.S. 133 (1914); Alabama, *Revised Code*, 1907, secs. 6846, 6848.

60. Baker, *Following the Color Line*, pp. 95–97; see also Jerome Dowd, *The Negro in American Life* (New York: Century, 1926), p. 132.

61. *State* v. *Etowah Lumber Co.* 153 Ala. 77 (1907).

62. *United States* v. *Reynolds* 235 U.S. 133 (1914).

63. Ibid.

64. Ibid.

*Chapter 6*

1. See case notes in the *Harvard Law Review* 24 (1911):391–95; *Columbia Law Review* 11 (1911):363–65; *Michigan Law Review* 11 (1912): 159–60.

2. *Report of the Attorney General of the United States* (1907), exhibit 17, p. 208.

3. Alabama, *Laws*, 1911, p. 93; South Carolina, *Acts*, 1912, no. 441; *State* v. *Armistead* 103 Miss. 790 (1913); *State* v. *Griffin* 154 N.C. 611 (1911).

4. Cited above, chapter 5, n. 49.

5. *Banks* v. *State* 124 Ga. 15 (1905); *Townsend* v. *State* 124 Ga. 69 (1905); *Lamar* v. *State* 120 Ga. 312 (1904); *Lamar* v. *Prosser* 121 Ga. 153 (1904); *Mulkey* v. *State* 1 Ga. App. 521 (1905).

6. *Latson* v. *Wells* 136 Ga. 681 (1911).

7. 138 Ga. 489 (1912); see also case note, *Michigan Law Review* 11 (1912):159.

8. *Wilson* v. *State* 138 Ga. 489 (1912).

9. Ibid.

10. Ibid.; Georgia was the only state to have such a rule.

11. Ibid.; *Bailey* v. *Alabama* 219 U.S. 219 (1911).

12. The court certainly did have a point when it noted that the jury would be under no obligation to believe the sworn testimony of such a witness, had such testimony been permitted. This was not only true, but highly likely, in the circumstances of such trials. The fact that the cards were already stacked, however, seems little excuse for blindfolding the "sucker."

13. See, for example, *Michigan Law Review* 11 (1912):159–60.

14. Florida, *Acts*, 1913, c. 6528, sec. 1.

15. *Goode* v. *Nelson* 73 Fla. 29 (1917).

16. Florida, *Acts*, 1919, c. 7917.

17. Chief Justice Browne, Associate Justices Ellis, Taylor, and Whitfield. See opinions in *Goode* v. *Nelson* 73 Fla. 29 (1917) and *Phillips* v. *Bell* 84 Fla. 233 (1922). (Whitfield and Taylor had also participated in an even earlier case, *Lewis* v. *Nelson* 62 Fla. 71 (1911), in which they denied the applicability of a fraud statute to a breach of contract by a laborer.)

18. *Phillips* v. *Bell* 84 Fla. 233 (1922); the case was brought up on appeal from a denial of a writ of habeas corpus.

19. Ibid. Separability was "adduced," however, on the grounds that "We cannot say that the legislature would not have enacted this law

without the provision [section 2] that certain facts should be *prima facie* evidence of the intent to injure and defraud."

20. See *State* v. *Hunter* 114 La. 939 (1905) (emphasis in the original).

21. See *State* v. *Breaux* 143 La. 653 (1918) and cases cited therein.

22. *State* v. *Oliva* 144 La. 51 (1918) (Bailey); *State* v. *Rout* 144 La. 53 (1918) (Rownd); *State* v. *Statham* 144 La. 54 (1918) (Rownd).

23. *State* v. *Murray* 116 La. 655 (1906), see above, chapter 5, n. 34.

24. North Carolina, *Revised Code*, 1935, c. 4482, refers to a Green County statute making it a misdemeanor for a cropper or tenant to break a contract without just cause and go to work for another. In forty-nine other counties in the state, a similar law was in effect (c. 4281).

25. *Johns* v. *Patterson* 138 Ark. 420 (1919); *State* v. *Moore* 166 Ark. 412 (1924); *State* v. *Nix* 165 Ala. 126 (1910); *Rhoden* v. *State* 161 Ga. 73 (1925); *State* v. *Hunter* 164 La. 405 (1927); *State* v. *Hurdle* 113 Miss. 736 (1917); *Hill* v. *Duckworth* 155 Miss. 491 (1929); *Waldrup* v. *State* 154 Miss. 647 (1929); and cases to be discussed below.

26. Arkansas, *Statutes*, 1919, sec. 5960; Alabama, *Revised Code*, 1928, secs. 3985, 3986, 3987; Florida, *Laws*, 1927, secs. 7166, 7177; Georgia, *Code*, 1926, secs. 123, 125; Louisiana, *Statutes*, 1932, vol. 3, sec. 4384, vol. 3, sec. 6606; Mississippi, *Code*, 1930, sec. 900; North Carolina, *Code*, 1931, secs. 4469, 4470; South Carolina, *Revised Code*, 1932, sec. 1314; Tennessee, *Revised Code*, 1932, secs. 8559, 8560. See also, Kentucky, *Statutes*, 1930, sec. 2601. (Kentucky, though not a Confederate state, had had an enticement law on its books since "slavery had been abolished in this state." See chapter 4, n. 49, above.)

27. *Shaw* v. *Fisher* 113 S.C. 287 (1919).

28. As noted earlier, this was based on the old English *Statute of Laborers* 23 Edw. III, c. 2, enacted in 1349, and long since repealed.

29. *Shaw* v. *Fisher* 113 S.C. 287 (1919); see case note in the *Yale Law Journal* 30 (1920): 174–76, for a discussion of the ruling.

30. 71 Miss. 509 (1893); see also, *Hoole* v. *Dorroh* 75 Miss. 257 (1897).

31. *Beale* v. *Yazoo Yarn Mill* 125 Miss. 807 (1921); *Shilling* v. *State* 143 Miss. 709 (1926); *Thompson* v. *Box* 147 Miss. 1 (1927).

32. *Thompson* v. *Box* 147 Miss. 1 (1927).

33. See, for example, Gunnar Myrdal, *An American Dilemma* (New York: Harper, 1944), p. 248 and passim.

34. See Pete Daniel, *The Shadow of Slavery: Peonage in the South, 1901–1969* (Urbana: University of Illinois Press, 1972), chapter 6. Daniel devotes almost a third of his study to this case and the Mississippi flood incident and examines both in great detail. After the end of the Wilson presidency, federal investigations of peonage picked up considerably,

but few cases were brought to trial, theoretically because the complaints were groundless.

35. Hugh M. Dorsey, *The Negro in Georgia* (Atlanta, Ga., 1921) in the Schomburg Collection, New York Public Library. Dorsey had just been defeated in a campaign for the Senate by Tom Watson, who was now an open (and rather vicious) racist.

36. Daniel, *Shadow of Slavery*, p. 128.

37. See *Crisis* 35 (1928): 1–110, for a full review of this incident. Also Daniel, *Shadow of Slavery*, chapter 8, passim.

38. Arthur F. Raper and Ira De A. Reid, *Sharecroppers All* (Chapel Hill: University of North Carolina Press, 1941); Thomas J. Woofter, *Landlord and Tenant on the Cotton Plantation* (Washington, D.C.: Bureau of Printing, 1936); Arthur F. Raper, *Preface to Peasantry* (Chapel Hill: University of North Carolina Press, 1936); Charles S. Johnson, *Shadow of the Plantation* (Chicago: University of Chicago Press, 1934).

39. *Taylor* v. *United States* 244 Fed. (S.C.) 321 (1917). The nonjudicial barriers, such as the failure of the Justice Department to assist in challenging the state court decisions in *Wilson* v. *State*, having been outlined above.

40. Ibid.

41. Ibid. At this point, sections 37 and 269 of the U.S. *Penal Code*.

42. Ibid. The court quoted *Clyatt* to this effect.

43. Ibid.

44. See Daniel, *Shadow of Slavery*, p. 80, fn. 52. Daniel mentions the case only in this footnote, and incorrectly states that the decision restored the South Carolina statute previously declared unconstitutional to a status of constitutionality. The law in question had been written after the *Bailey* decision, had never been challenged, and in any case, was never discussed in either the majority or the dissenting opinions. Daniel is meticulous in his description of the brutality and violence of any peonage incident he chooses to discuss, but is disappointingly casual and often inaccurate in detailing the legal aspects. To do him justice, while his information is largely drawn from Justice Department records, he does not claim to have produced a legal history of peonage; his interests lie in the social aspects of the practice.

*Chapter 7*

1. Office of the Attorney General, *Order No. 3204*, February 3, 1939.

2. See "Memorandum for the Attorney General, Re: Enforcement of Civil Liberties Statutes," issued on the same date as the order creating

the new section. (A copy of this memorandum was given to this writer by Professor John Elliff of Brandeis University.)

3. For discussion of these efforts, see Robert K. Carr, *Federal Protection of Civil Rights: Quest for a Sword* (Ithaca, N.Y.: Cornell University Press, 1947); Fred G. Folsom, Jr., "A Slave Trade Law in a Contemporary Setting," *Cornell Law Quarterly* 29 (1943–1944):203–16; Sydney Brodie, "The Federally Secured Right to be Free from Bondage," *Georgetown Law Journal* 40 (1952):367–98.

4. "Memorandum for the Attorney General," p. 2.

5. At this stage, the act was Section 444 of Title 18, *United States Code*. (Emphasis added.)

6. *Clyatt* v. *United States* 197 U.S. 207 (1905).

7. Charles W. Russell, *Report on Peonage* (Washington, D.C.: U.S. Department of Justice, 1908), p. 24; *United States* v. *Sabbia* (C.C.S.D. N.Y., 1907, unreported). Russell was badly outmaneuvered here, and Sabbia went free.

8. *United States* v. *Peacher* (E.D. Ark., 1937, unreported). Peacher had acquired the rights to clear some town land and cultivate it. He staffed the project by arresting all the blacks he could find, forcing them to plead guilty before the local justice of the peace (the mayor of the town). They were sentenced to hard labor on Peacher's new farm. See Donald H. Grubbs, *Cry from the Cotton: The Southern Tenant Farmer's Union and the New Deal* (Chapel Hill: University of North Carolina Press, 1971), p. 114.

9. At this time, Sec. 443, Title 18, *United States Code*.

10. Circular no. 3591, *Involuntary Servitude, Slavery and Peonage*, December 12, 1941. Biddle was the third attorney general in two years, as each of his predecessors, Frank Murphy and Robert Jackson, had been appointed to vacancies on the Supreme Court. This circular was striking in the precision of its language and the definitiveness of its instructions. It provides a primer for prosecution in these areas.

11. See William Henry Huff, "Peonage or Debt Slavery in the Land of the Free," *National Bar Journal* 3 (1945):47–48. Huff was a leading organizer of the committee. See also Pete Daniel, *The Shadow of Slavery: Peonage in the South, 1901–1969* (Urbana: University of Illinois Press, 1972), pp. 176–78.

12. *Taylor* v. *State* 191 Ga. 682 (1941).

13. *Taylor* v. *Georgia* 315 U.S. 25 (1942).

14. Ibid.

15. *United States* v. *Gaskin* 320 U.S. 527 (1944).

16. Ibid.

17. *Pollock* v. *Williams* 322 U.S. 4 (1944).

18. *Williams* v. *Pollock* 153 Fla. 338 (1943); *Phillips* v. *Bell* 84 Fla. 225 (1922), discussed in chapter 6.

19. *Pollock* v. *Williams* 322 U.S. 4 (1944).

20. Ibid. See chapter 6 for a discussion of this aspect of the Florida law.

21. Ibid. It is not clear what the interpretation of a substantive section which had never been contaminated by a prima facie clause would be—Jackson intimates it might be valid.

22. Ibid.

23. *United States* v. *Ingalls* 73 Fed. 76 (S.D. Cal. 1947).

24. U.S., Congress, Senate, Special Subcommittee on Labor and Labor-Management Relations, Committee on Labor and Public Welfare, *Labor Practices in Laurens County, Georgia*, 82d Cong., 1st sess., 1951, pp. 79–88.

25. U.S., Commission on Civil Rights, report no. 5, *Justice* (Washington, D.C., 1965), pp. 55, 203 n. 94. (These were generally contract law accusations and private convict-labor contracts.)

26. Harry H. Shapiro, "Involuntary Servitude: The Need for a More Flexible Approach," *Rutgers Law Review* 19 (1964):85.

27. Ibid.

28. *Justice*, p. 55.

### Conclusion

1. The historiographical "revolt" is discussed in the bibliographical note.

2. John P. Roche and Milton M. Gordon, "Can Morality Be Legislated," in Joel B. Grossman and Mary H. Grossman, eds., *Law and Change in Modern America* (Santa Monica, Calif.: Goodyear, 1971), pp. 245–51.

3. This is not to deny that other factors play a significant role—perhaps most strikingly, the likelihood of failure. See Michael Lipsky, "Protest as a Political Resource," in Kenneth M. Dolbeare, ed., *Power and Change in the United States* (New York: Wiley, 1969), pp. 161–78, for a discussion of this subject.

4. Roche and Gordon, "Morality," p. 249.

5. See U.S., Commission on Civil Rights, *Law Enforcement: A Report on Equal Protection in the South* (Washington, D.C.: Government Printing Office, 1965), pp. 89–91, for a discussion of sheriff's fees. See also, Charles V. Hamilton, *The Bench and the Ballot: Southern Federal Judges*

*and Black Voters* (New York: Oxford University Press, 1973), chapter 10, passim, for a discussion of economic penalties.

6. Harrell R. Rogers, Jr., and Charles S. Bullock III, *Law and Social Change* (New York: McGraw-Hill, 1972), p. 32. A full discussion of the operations and effectiveness of these provisions is found on pp. 15–66.

7. James E. Anderson, "Public Economy Policy and the Problem of Compliance: Notes for Research," in Grossman and Grossman, *Law and Change*, pp. 110–18.

8. For example, the record of the Justice Department in taking action on peonage complaints seems to be approached by one agency of the federal government—the National Labor Relations Board. The NLRB closed 86.5 percent of its cases *before* the issuance of a formal complaint. See Peter Woll, *Administrative Law: The Informal Process* (Berkeley: University of California Press, 1963), p. 127 and chapter 4, passim, for a review of agency action on complaint cases.

9. See Joel L. Grossman and Richard S. Wells, "The Concept of Judicial Policy-Making," *Journal of Public Law* 15 (1966): 287–310, for a full discussion of these factors.

10. Roche and Gordon, "Morality," p. 250.

# Bibliographical Note

*The prevailing note was one of tragedy.*

Claude Gernade Bowers

*What, then, constituted the alleged brutality that white southerners endured? First, the freeing of their slaves.*

Kenneth M. Stampp

Bernard A. Weisberger's phrase "The Dark and Bloody Ground of Reconstruction Historiography" (*Journal of Southern History* 25 [1959]:427–47) aptly reflects the intensity of an extraordinary scholarly dispute. Since the end of World War II, the accepted view of Reconstruction presented by the followers of Professor William A. Dunning, of Columbia University, has been stood on its head. This "Dunningite" approach had been the standard interpretation for most of the twentieth century, virtually without serious opposition in the field. The currently "accepted" writers are frankly known as "revisionists," and this title indicates the nature of the historiographical reversal which has taken place. The swing of the pendulum has been so complete that today the orthodoxy of Reconstruction seems to be without disciples. The change was not so swift as all that, to be sure, for there had been some voices in the dark as far back as the 1920s, but either metaphor gives an accurate notion of the level of general acceptance of the different views.

The orthodox view of Reconstruction told a simple story, filled with drama. The South, once the seat of gracious living and culture in America, is defeated in war, and devastation and poverty result. The careful, compassionate, and eminently sensible presidential Reconstruction plans, devised by Lincoln and nobly advanced and defended by Johnson, are destroyed when Congress is captured by a radical and vengeful minority who are determined to destroy the South and secure the economic and political dominance of the northern industrial states. Johnson is demeaned by impeachment and, though not convicted, is destroyed by the Radicals. At this point, the Radical Reconstruction of the South begins, with the South degraded and corrupted by the ignorant and often vicious rule of scalawags, illiterate Negroes, and northern carpetbaggers. The prostrate South endured this situation for some years and then, in a surge of revulsion, rose to destroy its tormentors. The rise of the Ku Klux Klan and its terror tactics was, perhaps, an overreaction, but clearly the white citizens had been forced into taking a united stand. By the late 1870s, even the North had become revolted at the corruption and decadence of Reconstruction rule and, after the disputed Hayes-Tilden election, the South was left to its own devices. Thus an experiment in corruption was abandoned, and the nation could breathe a sigh of relief and put its mistakes behind it.

This tale was not restricted to academe; it became part of the popular history of the nation and was, in its most vicious form, the basis of one of the most renowned films of all time: "The Birth of a Nation." Popular histories, such as Claude G. Bowers's *The Tragic Era*, further expanded the audience for the story, as did the novelizations of the glories of the Klan.

Doubtless there is, in the vast supply of source material on Reconstruction available to the historian, sufficient evidence to support the thesis, but, as current historians have shown, there is far more contrary material. As Vernon L. Wharton has noted ("Reconstruction," in Arthur S. Link and Rembert W. Patrick, eds., *Writing Southern History* [Baton Rouge: Louisiana State University Press, 1965]), with a vast array of sources to choose from, the historian can only "attempt to find the truth in terms of his own knowledge, conviction and values." Wharton goes on to ascribe the emergence of the Dunningite school to the social Darwinism of the period 1880–1910. The scholarly acceptance of white supremacy, as proven by science, and the defense of white Anglo-Saxon civilization against the hordes of immigrants and other lower races, was the background against which the Reconstruction scenario was written.

There were precursors of Dunning and his disciples, for Professor Dunning did not invent this interpretation but merely lent it academic verisimilitude. Professor Dunning himself published *Essays on the Civil War and Reconstruction and Related Topics* (New York: Macmillan, 1897) and *Reconstruction, Political and Economic: 1865–1877* (New York and London: Harper, 1907). He defended the Black Codes, grossly exaggerated black political influence and corruption, and excused or discounted the use of violence by whites. His view of the Negro in *Reconstruction* is typical: "The Negro had no pride of race and no aspirations or ideals save to be like the whites. With civil rights and political power, not won, but forced upon him, he came gradually to understand and crave those more elusive privileges that constitute social equality. A more intimate association with the other race . . . was the end toward which the ambition of the blacks tended . . . to direct itself." He asserted that this ambition had led to "the hideous crime against white womanhood which now assumed new meaning in the annals of outrage."

While Dunning's works were significant in themselves, his great influence lay in the works of his students, among whom were numbered such renowned scholars as James W. Garner, C. Mildred Thompson, Joseph G. de Roulhac Hamilton, and Walter L. Fleming. Although these and other scholars of the Dunningite school produced a vast monographic literature on Reconstruction, Fleming's two-volume *Documentary History of Reconstruction: Political, Military, Social, Religious, Educational and Industrial, 1865 to the Present Time* (Cleveland, Ohio: A. H. Clark, 1906–1907) was perhaps the most significant work insofar as it had the widest long-term effect on Reconstruction scholarship. A carefully selected body of brief pieces, these volumes clearly indicate the bias of the editor. As Wharton points out, the tendency of many historians to shy away from digging into original sources is well known, and Fleming enabled many of them to avoid that laborious task. Thus, for many years to come, much of the major "research" in Reconstruction history consisted of looking up the relevant passages in Fleming, which became a standard reference work in most libraries. Even the student with a reasonable degree of skepticism about the orthodox view of the period frequently based his arguments on sources that reinforced that view.

In the period when the Dunning students were publishing

and solidifying their interpretation, the only opposition they had to face was the work of blacks. John R. Lynch, Alrutheus Ambush Taylor and W. E. B. DuBois all attacked the Dunning thesis, but were, by and large, ignored by the academic world. DuBois suffered particularly from his failure to examine original sources and was straining credulity with his interpretations of the materials he used. It took some doing to disprove the Dunningites when using Fleming's *Documentary History* as a major source. Further, he insisted on viewing the period through a Marxist glass, which was ill fitted for the task.

The story of the beginnings of the successful revolution in Reconstruction historiography has been well told. Vernon L. Wharton, Richard N. Current, Bernard A. Weisberger, and many others have described the calls for a new emphasis on basic research by Howard K. Beale and Francis B. Simkins in the early thirties; they have also recorded the successes of Horace Mann Bond and others. While the revisionist interpretation has become as pervasive and ubiquitous as the Dunning view once was, it is not clear that the call for new and basic research on source materials has always been answered. Much of the revisionist material has been merely an attempt to fit the old facts into a new mold.

Perhaps even more distressing is the common tendency to play by the Dunningites' rules. That is, the parameters of the dispute have been set by the revisionists' understandable desire to answer and contradict the historians of the old school. As a result, those subjects most emphasized by their predecessors are given similar treatment by the revisionists. This factor, more than any other, may best explain the lack of scholarly interest in subjects like peonage.

In recent years there has been an emergence of works whose authors are going back to original sources. The area of economics (and within this field, agricultural economics) has been particularly rich in fresh scholarly articles, but history has seen a revival in this regard as well. Only a percentage of this material is of relevance to a legal study of peonage, however, and therefore a survey of this literature will not be attempted here.

C. Vann Woodward's *Origins of the New South* (Baton Rouge: Louisiana State University Press, 1951) is required reading for any student of southern politics and history. Similarly, Vernon L. Wharton's *The Negro in Mississippi, 1865–1890* (Chapel Hill: University of North Carolina Press, 1947) remains a superlatively documented account of the period.

While George R. Bentley's *History of the Freedmen's Bureau* (Philadelphia: University of Pennsylvania Press, 1955) is merely a restatement of Paul Pierce's 1904 work, William S. McFeely's admirable biography of O. O. Howard, *Yankee Stepfather: General O. O. Howard and the Freedmen* (New Haven, Conn., and London: Yale University Press, 1968), presents a fresh and intelligent reinterpretation of the bureau and its works. (Interestingly, McFeely places great emphasis on the labor contract.) Further, *The Freedmen's Bureau in South Carolina, 1865–1872*, by Martin L. Abbott (Chapel Hill: University of North Carolina Press, 1967), is an excellent state study which examines the day-to-day operations of the bureau.

Theodore B. Wilson's *The Black Codes of the South* (Birmingham: University of Alabama Press, 1965) seems to fill the crying need for a study of these laws. On closer examination, however, the zealous (and rather unconvincing) defense of the South's posture on the codes tends to make the selections used somewhat less credible. It is, however, the only work that deals extensively with these laws, and it does provide some healthy quotations from them.

Joel Williamson's *After Slavery: The Negro in South Carolina during Reconstruction, 1861–1877* (Chapel Hill: University of North Carolina Press, 1963) is a uniquely interesting book, derived from plantation records. It provides a much-needed description of the everyday life and relationships of the freedmen and planters. Of similar interest is Willie Lee Rose's *Rehearsal for Reconstruction: The Port Royal Experiment* (Indianapolis: University of Indiana Press, 1965) which concentrates on the Sea Islands of South Carolina, where a unique experiment of northern and freedman cooperation took place. The book is eminently readable, but the Sea Islands situation was by no means typical in the context of the rest of the South.

George B. Tindall's *South Carolina Negroes, 1877–1890* (New York: Columbia University Press, 1952) is a less useful study of that state than the Williamson work noted above, but one chapter is devoted to a reasonable, albeit sketchy, discussion of labor-contract and lien laws.

There is a visible trend towards new attempts to research the period. From the point of view of this study, the great failing is the insistent concentration on the same areas of interest which the Dunning school put forward and the feeling that there is no need to do more than dispute their conclusions. I would contend that race prejudice in the South can now be accepted as proven, that in academe at least, the debarment of Negro suffrage on grounds of inherent racial inferiority may be considered a dead issue, and that the historian may now fully turn his attention to those areas of social, political, and economic history which have lain dormant for almost a century.

In this latter context, the study of peonage stands out as a striking example of neglect. There are two studies, however, which do provide some insight into the subject. Howard Devon Hamilton's doctoral dissertation, "The Legislative and Judicial History of the Thirteenth Amendment" (Urbana: University of Illinois Press, 1950) provides the only significant legal discussion of the problem, albeit in short form, as the question of peonage is only a side issue in the study. Further, Hamilton naturally only becomes interested in the problem when the Thirteenth Amendment becomes a useful tool to combat it, thereby ignoring the period 1865–1900. Nonetheless, it remains the most valuable work extant on this subject.

Pete Daniel's *The Shadow of Slavery: Peonage in the South, 1901–1969* (Urbana: University of Illinois Press, 1972) is a book wholly devoted to peonage. It is a useful and readable book, despite the fact that it concentrates on a few of the more spectacular and dramatic cases of this century as indicators of the whole process. However, Daniel is a bit fuzzy in his (few) legal interpretations; he is forced to ignore the origins of the practice, and the study resolutely ignores the bedfellows of debt-slavery—namely, enticement laws, convict labor, and so on. This last failing is, I think, the most serious and makes it impossible to get a realistic picture of the whole process of forced labor in the South.

William Delmer Wagoner's unpublished dissertation on peonage, "The Non-Free Worker in Post-Civil War American History" (University of Texas, 1961) is subject to many of the faults attributed to the early revisionist literature—that is, he tries to prove his points without incorporating any original research.

Dan T. Carter, "Prisons, Politics and Business: The Convict Lease System in the Post–Civil War South" (M.A. thesis, University of Wisconsin, 1964) is a valuable bibliographical source for materials on convict leasing, but less valuable when dealing with legal structures that made that system possible.

The legal sources used in this study were basically the collected statutes and cases of the various states involved. As Shepard's *Indexes* proved inadequate as citators for the pre-1900 period, the *Century Digest* became a major source of cases, as did Labatt, *Master and Servant*, a massive turn-of-the-century study of master-servant relationships in American law. With the exception of a few law journal "notes," the bulk of the legal research consisted of a determined plodding through the statutes and cases of the period. In brief, peonage still represents a subject area much in need of documentation and research. Original materials are available, but secondary sources are few and often suspect.

# Index